UNDERSTANDING SOCIOLOGY

◆◆◆

A Student Workbook for Active Learning

Revised Edition

Yolaine Armand

University of Cincinnati

LONGMAN

An Imprint of Addison Wesley Longman, Inc

New York • Reading, Massachusetts • Menlo Park, California • Harlow, England
Don Mills, Ontario • Sydney • Mexico City • Madrid • Amsterdam

Addison Wesley Longman Custom Books consist of products that are produced from camera-ready copy. Peer review, class testing, and accuracy are primarily the responsibility of the author(s).

Manager of Addison Wesley Longman Custom Books: Caralee Woods
Production Administrator: Liz Faerm
Cover Design: Zina Scarpulla

UNDERSTANDING SOCIOLOGY:
A STUDENT WORKBOOK FOR ACTIVE LEARNING
Revised Edition

Copyright © 1997 by Yolaine Armand

All rights reserved. Printed in the United States of America. No part of this book may be used or reproduced in any manner whatsoever without written permission from the publisher except testing materials, which may be copied for classroom use. For information, address Addison Wesley Educational Publishers Inc., 1185 Avenue of the Americas, New York, New York 10036.

ISBN: 0-201-32237-4

97 98 99 3 2 1

CONTENTS

To The Student	iii
Reading for Comprehension	v
Introduction	vii

1 SOCIOLOGY - THE DISCIPLINE

Objectives	1
Understanding Your Own Textbook Reading	2
Testing Your Knowledge	5
Essay Practice	8
Critical Thinking Exercises	9
Invitation to Sociology: Peter L. Berger	11

2 DOING RESEARCH IN SOCIOLOGY

Objectives	15
Understanding Your Own Textbook Reading	16
Essay Practice	19
Critical Thinking Exercises	20
Project	21
The Promise of Sociology: C. Wright Mills	23

3 CULTURE

Objectives	29
Understanding Your Own Textbook Reading	30
Testing Your Knowledge	33
Essay Practice	36
Critical Thinking Exercises	37
Additional Reading and Special Project	38
A World View of Cultural Diversity: Thomas Sowell	39

4 SOCIETIES AND SOCIAL STRUCTURE

Objectives	43
Understanding Your Own Textbook Reading	44
Testing Your Knowledge	47
Essay Practice	50
Critical Thinking Exercises	51

5 SOCIALIZATION

Objectives	53
Understanding Your Own Textbook Reading	54
Testing Your Knowledge	56
Essay Practice	60
Critical Thinking Exercises	61
My Daughter Smokes: Alice Walker	63

6 GROUPS AND ORGANIZATIONS

Objectives	67
Understanding Your Own Textbook Reading	68
Testing Your Knowledge	71
Essay Practice	74
Critical Thinking Exercises	75
Slim's Table: Mitchell Duneier	77

7 DEVIANCE, CRIME, AND SOCIAL CONTROL

Objectives	81
Understanding Your Own Textbook Reading	82
Testing Your Knowledge	84
Essay Practice	87
Critical Thinking Exercises	88
Differential Association: Edwin H. Sutherland	89

8 SOCIAL STRATIFICATION

Objectives	93
Understanding Your Own Textbook Reading	94
Testing Your Knowledge	96
Essay Practice	99
Critical Thinking Exercises	100
Some Principles of Stratification: Kingsley Davis and Wilbert E. Moore	101

9 WORLD STRATIFICATION

Objectives	105
Understanding Your Own Textbook Reading	106
Testing Your Knowledge	108
Essay Practice	111
Critical Thinking Exercises	112

10 RACE AND ETHNIC RELATIONS

Objectives	115
Understanding Your Own Textbook Reading	116
Testing Your Knowledge	118
Essay Practice	121
Critical Thinking Exercises	122
Racism: Denial and Perpetuation: Martin Lee and Norman Solomon	123

11 SEX, GENDER, AND SOCIETY

Objectives	131
Understanding Your Own Textbook Reading	132
Testing Your Knowledge	135
Essay Practice	137
Projects and Critical Thinking Exercises	138
Why It's So Tough to be a Girl: Nancy J. Perry	139

TO THE STUDENT

This workbook is designed to facilitate your comprehension of sociology and to get you interested in a science that impacts on every aspect of every person's life. Whether or not you are a sociology major, you cannot escape from the influence of the social system, so your being an informed participant in the social drama, and not a mere spectator, will prove to be beneficial in many ways.

This workbook is further dedicated to the proposition that active learning is more rewarding to the learner, and results in longer-lasting benefits, than passive learning.

Active learning involves taking responsibility for the learning process, establishing learning goals, and pursuing them intelligently. It involves using critical thinking, the capacity to analyze what is proposed, to determine its usefulness, its strengths as well as its limitations. Active learning involves linking what you learn to your personal experiences and to situations that may be familiar to you. It involves using the "sociological imagination," seeing the connection between the individual and the social system. It finally involves learning from each other and sharing your thoughts with others.

This workbook is intended to do the following:

- Guide you through reading the textbook on a weekly basis.

- Highlight important concepts and provide reinforcement for their comprehension, application, and retention.

- Help integrate your learning to your everyday life by encouraging you to think critically.

- Provide additional readings for further thinking and enhanced understanding.

How to Use the Workbook

Use your workbook as you do your textbook reading assignments. DO YOUR ASSIGNMENT EVERY WEEK, BEFORE COMING TO CLASS. First read the objectives carefully, study the questions, and try to think of what you would like to know about the topic. As you read the material, fill out the part "Understanding Your Textbook Reading," then test yourself with the "True and False" and "Multiple Choice" questions. The essay questions give you a chance to practice your writing skills in preparation for exams, and to reinforce the major concepts presented in your textbook. Check your book for the correct answer, then practice writing in your own words. Finally, the "Critical Thinking Exercises" and other projects have to be done in the same week. You may be asked to write some notes and come prepared for class discussion or small group exercises, or to turn in the project in writing, after discussing it in class. The additional readings will provide material for further classroom discussion and utilization.

Some General Advice

1. Set aside some specific time for uninterrupted study on a **regular basis**.

2. Before you read each chapter, try to "tune in" by reflecting on the topic for a few minutes and coming up with some questions of your own.

3. Do your reading in separate blocks of time, if you find this more convenient. Divide the material in several segments and try to summarize the major parts of each segment before you go on to the next one.

4. Always scan the material to get an overall view of the general content. Look at the forest before you look at the trees: this will facilitate your reading for comprehension.

5. SCAN--THINK--READ--REFLECT--SUMMARIZE--APPLY. Practice the ST 2R SA method.

6. Read for comprehension by trying to relate the unknown to the familiar. Try to see some applications to the concepts you are learning.

7. Check any new word in the dictionary: you will improve your vocabulary, while getting a clearer understanding of the material.

8. Write as you read: underline, divide, number, use your "NOTES" pages freely. Your workbook will facilitate your review for exams.

Make learning a partnership between you, the textbook author, your instructor, and your classmates.

ABOVE ALL, ENJOY YOUR ACTIVE LEARNING.

READING FOR COMPREHENSION

Getting Acquainted With Your Syllabus

1. Write down the following information:

    a. title of the course:
    b. course number:
    c. name of the instructor (check correct spelling):

2. What topics will be covered?

    a. the fourth week of class?

    b. the seventh week of class?

    c. the tenth week of class?

3. Of all the topics listed, which one is your favorite and why?

4. What is the difference between the course <u>overview</u> and the course <u>objectives</u>? (Use complete sentences.)

5. List the dates of all exams (and quizzes), including the final.

6. List three specific knowledge/understanding items you would like to gain about society.

7. Of the class requirements listed, which one will be easiest for your to fulfill? Which one will be the hardest?

8. What is your overall objective for this course (beside "learning everything about sociology or society")?

9. From the course objectives listed in your syllabus, write down the one which is the most important to <u>you</u> and explain why in a short paragraph. Rank all the other objectives in order of importance to you. Add your own objective(s) if you so desire.

10. General comments:

INTRODUCTION

Getting Acquainted With Your Textbook

Prepare yourself for intelligent reading by becoming familiar with your assigned textbook. First preview the entire text as you answer the following questions.

1. Write the book's author(s), its title, publisher, and year of publication:

2. How many <u>parts</u> are there in the book? _____
   List the different titles in the order in which they appear in the book:

3. List the titles of the book <u>chapters</u>.

4. Using the <u>glossary</u> at the <u>end</u> of the textbook, write down the definitions of the following terms:

   anomie:

   deviance (or deviant behavior):

   ethnocentrism:

   society:

   socialization:

5. From the bibliography given in your textbook, select five (or more) books you would like to read for more information. List these books by author and title.

    1.

    2.

    3.

    4.

    5.

Now that you have taken a look at the "forest" (the whole book), you may begin to look at the "trees" (individual chapters).

CHAPTER 1

Sociology - The Discipline

Objectives

This chapter introduces Sociology as a distinct social science and not a mere collection of common sense about people. It retraces the origin of the new science, its early development in Europe and the U.S., and the major contributions of the social scientists who have shaped its content and methodology.

Here are some questions you may want to raise:

1. What is sociology? Is it not a collection of common sense explanations of what happens in society?

2. How is sociology different from the other social sciences?

3. I am not a sociology major; what can knowledge of sociology do for me?

4. What socio-economic or political factors contributed to the emergence of the new science?

5. Who were the original thinkers whose ideas shaped the development of sociology?

6. Can sociology improve society? How?

7. Can sociology help individuals as well as societies? If so, how?

Your own questions:

UNDERSTANDING YOUR OWN TEXTBOOK READING

1. Define sociology and write down at least ten topics relevant to the field:

2. The term "sociological imagination" was described by
   _____ and refers to
   _____.

3. Discuss the major social factors that were at the origin of the development of European sociology in the nineteenth century.

4. Explain the difference between the social sciences and the natural sciences.

5. Name the early European thinkers who influenced the development of sociology. Describe three important contributions made by each one of them.

6. Identify the early American sociologists. Describe the contributions of the three you consider most influential.

7. How did early American sociologists view the purpose of sociology? How does that compare to European sociology?

8. A perspective (or paradigm), in sociology, can be defined as:

   and the three major sociological perspectives are called:

9. The conflict perspective states that societies are organized the way they are because:

10. Indicate at least ten examples of conflict of interests (or competition) that can be found in our society:

11. Find five words which are crucial in the definition of the symbolic interactionist perspective:

   1.
   2.
   3.
   4.
   5.

   How would you define the symbolic interactionist perspective using these five words?

12. List the names of American sociologists from the interactionist perspective and briefly describe their major ideas:

13. Of the three sociological perspectives, which one(s) is (are) macro- and microsociological? Explain why.

14. Write your own assessment of the three sociological perspectives. How do they view society and social problems? How useful is each one to you In trying to understand daily occurrences?

TESTING YOUR KNOWLEDGE

True and False

1. The authors of the textbook are sociology professors at Michigan State University.   T F

2. Part One consists of chapters 1, 2, 3, and 4.   T F

3. The term "sociology" was used about 1,000 years ago.   T F

4. Sociology as a discipline first emerged in Europe.   T F

5. Social science can predict behavior based on scientific measurement.   T F

6. Sociology is a problem-solving tool.   T F

7. Sociology can be applied to only a limited number of social issues and concerns.   T F

8. The three sociological perspectives offer different explanations for human behavior.   T F

9. Emile Durkheim had no major influence in the development of the functionalist perspective.   T F

10. The functionalist perspective emphasizes order and stability.   T F

11. According to the conflict perspective, the particular characteristics of any given society were developed because they met the needs of that society.   T F

12. The conflict perspective is a microsociological perspective.   T F

13. Conflict is another word for violence. They are the same.   T F

14. Conflict theorists see conflict as natural, normal, and useful to society.   T F

15. A manifest function is a function of a social arrangement that is not evident and is often unintended.   T F

16. All three sociological perspectives analyze society at the macro level.   T F

17. Symbols and meanings are important components of the conflict perspective.   T F

18. Latent functions are unintended consequences.   T F

Multiple Choice

1. _____ is credited for being the founder of sociology.

    a. Karl Marx
    b. August Comte
    c. Max Weber
    d. C. Wright Mills

2. Sociology was first developed in America: _____

    a. in Chicago
    b. at UCLA
    c. at Harvard
    d. at Columbia

3. The concept of the "sociological imagination" was developed by: _____

    a. Auguste Comte
    b. Karl Marx
    c. C. Wright Mills
    d. Emile Durkheim

4. The principle that science accepts nothing on the basis of faith or common sense is called: _____

    a. scientific inquiry
    b. rationalization
    c. organized skepticism
    d. scientific explanation

5. The first sociologist to do an in-depth, systematic study of suicide is: _____

    a. Auguste Comte
    b. Emile Durkheim
    c. Robert Merton
    d. None of the above

6. Sociology differs from the other social sciences because of its emphasis on: _____

    a. individuals
    b. values
    c. society
    d. past civilizations

7. Which of the following do sociologists study? _____

    a. social groups and their functions
    b. social institutions
    c. the way people learn how to behave in society
    d. all of the above

8. Which of the following is not a social science? _____

   a. Anthropology
   b. Economics
   c. Geology
   d. Psychology

9. An early woman pioneer in the development of sociology in Europe was: _____

   a. Harriet Martineau
   b. Jane Adams
   c. Carol Brooks Gardner
   d. Frances Heussenstamm

10. According to conflict theorists, conflict is useful to society because it makes possible: _____

    a. the disruption of the social order
    b. social change
    c. the maintenance of the *status quo*
    d. social dysfunctions

ESSAY PRACTICE

1. Describe some of the positive and negative effects of "globalization" on the American economy and on popular culture.

2. Compare sociology to three other social sciences. Show the common grounds and the differences.

3. What are the key principles of the functionalist and conflict perspectives? Give a comprehensive summary of each in no more than two or three sentences.

CRITICAL THINKING EXERCISES

1. Analyze the following issues, applying the "sociological perspective" to explain what is happening in our society today.

   - The abortion controversy
   - The high divorce rate in our society
   - Your pursuit of a college education
   - The high rate of crime in urban areas
   - The growing number of the poor and homeless in the midst of affluence
   - The increase in the number of one-parent households

2. Discuss the careers open to sociology majors. How can knowledge of sociology help the non-sociology major?

3. Show how you would use either the functionalist, conflict, or symbolic interactionist perspective to best explain the following:

   - A bus driver's strike
   - Entrance requirements at U.S. Ivy League schools
   - The high cost of medical studies
   - The popular outrage over the flag-burning issue
   - The Supreme Court ruling on abortion
   - Waves of racism in various American communities

   Two additional contemporary social issues of your choice:

   -

   -

4. How have feminist scholars and people of color enhanced our understanding of human behavior?

INVITATION TO SOCIOLOGY
Peter L. Berger

The SOCIOLOGIST (that is, the one we would really like to invite to our game) is a person intensively, endlessly, shamelessly interested in the doings of men. His natural habitat is all the human gathering places of the world, wherever men come together. The sociologist may be interested in many other things. But his consuming interest remains in the world of men, their institutions, their history, their passions. And since he is interested in men, nothing that men do can be altogether tedious for him. He will naturally be interested in the events that engage men's ultimate beliefs, their moments of tragedy and grandeur and ecstasy. But he will also be fascinated by the commonplace, the everyday. He will know reverence, but his reverence will not prevent him from wanting to see and to understand. He may sometimes feel revulsion or contempt. But this also will not deter him from wanting to have his questions answered. The sociologist, in his quest for understanding, moves through the world of men without respect for the usual lines of demarcation. Nobility and degradation, power and obscurity, intelligence and folly--these are equally *interesting* to him, however unequal they may be in his personal values or tastes. Thus his questions may lead him to all possible levels of society, the best and the least known places, the most respected and the most despised. And, if he is a good sociologist, he will find himself in all these places because his own questions have so taken possession of him that he has little choice but to seek for answers.

It would be possible to say the same things in a lower key. We could say that the sociologist, but for the grace of his academic title is the man who must listen to gossip despite himself, who is tempted to look through keyholes, to read other people's mail, to open cabinets. Before some otherwise unoccupied psychologist sets out now to construct an aptitude test for sociologists on the basis of sublimated voyeurism, let us quickly say that we are speaking merely by way of analogy. Perhaps some little boys consumed with curiosity to watch their maiden aunts in the bathroom later become inveterate sociologists. This is quite uninteresting. What interests us is the curiosity that grips any sociologist in front of a closed door behind which there are human voices. If he is a good sociologist he will want to open that door, to understand these voices. Behind each closed door he will anticipate some new facet of human life not yet perceived and understood.

The sociologist will occupy himself with matters that others regard as too sacred or as too distasteful for dispassionate investigation. He will find rewarding the company of priests or of prostitutes, depending not on his personal preferences but on the questions he happens to be asking at the moment. He will also concern himself with matters that others may find much too boring. He will be interested in the human interaction that goes with warfare or with great intellectual discoveries, but also in the relations between people employed in a restaurant or between a group of little girls playing with their dolls. His main focus of attention is not the ultimate significance of what men do, but the action in itself as another example of the infinite richness of human conduct. So much for the image of playmate.

In these journeys through the world of men the sociologist will inevitably encounter other professional Peeping Toms. Sometimes these will resent his presence, feeling that he is poaching on their preserves. In some places the sociologist will meet up with the economist, in others with the political scientist, in yet others with the psychologist or the ethnologist. Yet chances are that the questions that have brought him to these places are different from the ones that propelled his fellow-trespassers. The sociologist's questions always remain essentially the same: "What are these people doing with each other here?" "What are their relationships to each other?" "How are these relationships organized in institutions?" "What are the collective ideas that move men and institutions?" In trying to answer these questions in specific instances, the sociologist will, of course, have to deal with economic or political matters, but he will do so in a way rather different from that of the economist or the political scientist. The scene that he contemplates is the same human scene that these other scientists concern themselves with. But the sociologist's angle of vision is different.

When this is understood, it becomes clear that it makes little sense to try to stake out a special enclave within which the sociologist will carry on business in his own right. Like Wesley the sociologist will have to confess that his parish is the world. But unlike some latter-day Wesleyans he will gladly share this parish with others. There is, however, one traveler whose path the sociologist will cross more often than anyone else's on his journeys. This is the historian. Indeed, as soon as the sociologist turns from the present to the past, his preoccupations are vary hard indeed to distinguish from those of the historian. [T]he sociological journey will be much impoverished unless it is punctuated frequently by conversation with that other particular traveler.

Any intellectual activity derives excitement from the moment it becomes a trail of discovery...The excitement of sociology is [not always to penetrate] into worlds that had previously been quite unknown...for instance, the world of crime, or the world of some bizarre religious sect, or the world fashioned by the exclusive concerns of some group such as medical specialists or military leaders or advertising executives. [M]uch of the time the sociologist moves in sectors of experience that are familiar to him and to most people in his society. He investigates communities, institutions, and activities that one can read about every day in the newspapers. Yet there is another excitement of discovery beckoning in his investigations. It is not the excitement of finding the familiar becoming transformed in its meaning. The fascination of sociology lies in the fact that its perspective makes us see in a new light the very world in which we have lived all of our lives. This also constitutes a transformation of consciousness. Moreover, this transformation is more relevant existentially that that of many other intellectual disciplines, because it is more difficult to segregate in some special compartment of the mind. The astronomer does not live in the remote galaxies, and the nuclear physicist can, outside his laboratory, eat and laugh, and marry, and vote without thinking about the insides of the atom. The geologist looks at rocks only at appropriate times, and the linguist speaks English with his wife. The sociologist lives in society, on the job and off it. His own life, inevitably, is part of his subject matter. Men being what they are, sociologists too manage to segregate their professional insights from their everyday affairs. But it is a rather difficult feat to perform in good faith.

The sociologist moves in the common world of men, close to what most of them would call real. The categories he employs in his analyses are only refinements of the categories by which other men live--power, class, status, race, ethnicity. As a result, there is a deceptive simplicity and obviousness about some sociological investigations. One reads them, nods at the familiar scene, remarks that one has heard all this before and don't people have better things to do than to waste their time on truisms--until one is suddenly brought up against an insight that radically questions everything one had previously assumed about this familiar scent. This is the point at which one begins to sense the excitement of sociology.

Let us take a specific example. Imagine a sociology class in a Southern college where almost all the students are white Southerners. Imagine a lecture on the subject of the racial system of the South. The lecturer is talking here of matters that have been familiar to his students from the time of their infancy. Indeed, it may be that they are much more familiar with the minutiae of this system than he is. They are quite bored as a result. It seems to them that he is only using more pretentious words to describe what they already know. Thus he may use the term "caste", one commonly used now by traditional Hindu society, to make it clearer. He then goes on to analyze the magical beliefs inherent in caste tabus, the social dynamics of commensalism and connubium, the economic interests concealed within the system, the way in which religious beliefs relate to the tabus, the effects of the cast system upon the industrial development of the society and vice versa--all in India. But suddenly India is not very far away at all. The lecture then goes back to its Southern theme. The familiar now seems not quite so familiar anymore. Questions are raised that are new, perhaps raised angrily, but raised all the same. And at least some of the students have begun to understand that there are functions involved in this business of race that they have not read about in the newspapers (at least not those in their hometowns) and that their parents have not told them--partly, at least, because neither the newspapers nor the parents knew about them

It can be said that the first wisdom of sociology is this--things are not what they seem. This too is a deceptively simple statement. It ceases to be simple after a while. Social reality turns out to have many layers of meaning. The discovery of each new layer changes the perception of the whole.

Anthropologists use the term "culture shock" to describe the impact of a totally new culture upon a newcomer. In an extreme instance such shock will be experienced by the Western explorer who is told, halfway through dinner, that he is eating the nice old lady he had been chatting with the previous day--a shock with predictable physiological if not moral consequences. Most explorers no longer encounter cannibalism in their travels today. However, the first encounters with polygamy or with puberty rites or even with the way some nations view their automobiles can be quite a shock to an American visitor. With the shock may go not only disapproval or disgust but a sense of excitement that things can *really* be that different from what they are at home. To some extent, at least, this is the excitement of any first travel abroad. The experience of sociological discovery could be described as "culture shock" minus geographical displacement. In other words, the sociologist travels at home--with shocking results. He is unlikely to find that he is eating a nice old lady for dinner. But the discovery, for instance, that his own church has considerable money invested in the missile industry or that a few blocks from his home there are people who engage in cultic orgies may not be drastically different in emotional impact. Yet we would not want to imply that sociological discoveries are always or even usually outrageous to moral sentiment. Not at all. What they have in common with exploration in distant lands, however, is the sudden illumination of new and unsuspected facets of human existence in society...

People who like to avoid shocking discoveries, who prefer to believe that society is just what they were taught in Sunday school, who like the safety of the rules and the maxims of what Alfred Schutz has called the "world-taken-for-granted", should stay away from sociology. People who feel no temptation before closed doors, who have no curiosity about human beings, who are content to admire scenery without wondering about the people who live in those houses on the other side of that river, should probably stay away from sociology. They will find it unpleasant or, at any rate, unrewarding. People who are interested in human beings only if they can change, convert, or reform them should also be warned, for they will find sociology much less useful than they had hoped. And people whose interest is mainly in their own conceptual constructions will do just as well to turn to the study of little white mice. Sociology will be satisfying, in the long run, only to those who can think of nothing more entrancing than to watch men and to understand things human.

It may now be clear that we have, albeit deliberately, understated the case in the title of this chapter. [The chapter title from which this selection is taken is "Sociology as an Individual Pastime."] To be sure, sociology is an individual pastime in the sense that it interests some men and bores others. Some like to observe human beings, others to experiment with mice. The world is big enough to hold all kinds and there is no logical priority for one interest as against another. But the word "pastime" is weak in describing what we mean. Sociology is more like a passion. The sociological perspective is more like a demon that possesses one, that drives one compellingly, again and again, to the questions that are its own. And introduction to sociology is, therefore, an invitation to a very special kind of passion. ■

1. Name at least ten topics that a sociologist would be interested in studying. What do they all have in common? How would the sociologist's point of view differ from that of the other professional "peeping Toms" mentioned by the author?

2. How does the sociologist view the familiar scene, the obvious? Give an example.

NOTES

CHAPTER 2

Doing Research in Sociology

Objectives

Through this chapter, you will familiarize yourself with the methods used in scientific research by sociologists and other social scientists.

Here are some of the questions you may want to raise:

1. What methods are used in scientific inquiry? What are the usefulness and limitations of each?

2. What steps should I take to do research on a particular sociological topic? How would I investigate this topic using the methods of sociology?

3. What is the role of values in scientific research? How would my own values affect the kind of research I undertake and the kind of conclusions I reach?

4. How would I go about researching a topic of interest to me? Where do I start? How do I proceed? What resources are available to me? What methodology?

Your own questions:

UNDERSTANDING YOUR OWN TEXTBOOK READING

1. Scientists do research in order to _____,
   or to _____, or to _____ (use verbs).
   Add as many additional verbs as you can think about and which appear relevant.

2. A hypothesis is _____.
   (Do not define as "an educated guess".)

3. Give one example each (your own) of:

    a. a statement indicating a value judgment:

    b. a sociological question:

    c. a sociological concept:

   What is the difference between the three?

4. What is the difference between validity and reliability?

5. Describe the Hawthorne experiment and the conclusive "Hawthorne Effect."

6. A variable is _____.

   An independent variable is _____.

   A dependent variable is _____.

   The variable _____ is thought of as the cause, and the _____ variable is seen as the result.

7. In the following hypothesis, identify the independent and dependent variables:

   "As people's level of education increases, their level of prejudice tends to decrease."

   Independent variable: _____

   Dependent variable: _____

8. Give operational definitions of the two variables in question #7.

   a. _____

   b. _____

9. Is the correlation in the above-mentioned hypothesis positive or negative? _____
   Why?

10. Give an example of a spurious relationship:

11. List the key research methods in sociology:

12. What types of data sources can be used in sociological research?

13. What is content analysis?

14. What is the difference between participant observation and unobtrusive observation?

15. Summarize the basic principles of ethics in social research:

ESSAY PRACTICE

Establish the difference between <u>experiments</u>, <u>surveys</u>, and <u>observations</u> as primary data collection techniques (research methods) used by social scientists. List their respective advantages, pitfalls, and disadvantages.

CRITICAL THINKING EXERCISES

For each data gathering technique (research design), list three sociological topics that can be investigated by the method. Explain how.

PROJECT

Select one sociological topic of interest to you.

    a.   State the topic:

    b.   List three questions you would like to answer about your topic:

        b.1. _____

        b.2. _____

        b.3. _____

    c.   What kind of hypothesis could you formulate?

    d.   How would you apply the steps of the scientific method to research your topic?

    e.   What research design would be more appropriate to your study? Why?

    f.   Justify the nature of your research: whether descriptive or designed to test a hypothesis, qualitative, or quantitative.

THE PROMISE OF SOCIOLOGY
C. Wright Mills

Nowadays men often feel that their private lives are a series of traps. They sense that within their everyday worlds, they cannot overcome their troubles, and in this feeling, they are often quite correct: what ordinary men are directly aware of and what they try to do are bounded by the private orbits in which they live; their visions and their powers are limited to the close-up scenes of job, family, neighborhood; in other milieux, they move vicariously and remain spectators. And the more aware they become, however vaguely, of ambitions and of threats which transcend their immediate locales, the more trapped they seem to feel.

Underlying this sense of being trapped are seemingly impersonal changes in the very structure of continent-wide societies. The facts of contemporary history are also facts about the success and the failure of individual men and women. When a society is industrialized, a peasant becomes a worker; a feudal lord is liquidated or becomes a businessman. When classes rise or fall, a man is employed or unemployed; when the rate of investment goes up or down, a man takes new heart or goes broke. When wars happen, an insurance salesman becomes a rocket launcher; a store clerk, a radar man; a wife lives alone; a child grows up without a father. Neither the life of an individual nor the history of a society can be understood without understanding both.

Yet men do not usually define the troubles they endure in terms of historical change and institutional contradiction. The well-being they enjoy, they do not usually impute to the big ups and downs of the societies in which they live. Seldom aware of the intricate connection between the patterns of their own lives and the course of world history, ordinary men do not usually know what this connection means for the kinds of men they are becoming and for the kinds of history-making in which they might take part. They do not possess the quality of mind essential to grasp the interplay of man and society, of biography and history, of self and world. They cannot cope with their personal troubles in such ways as to control the structural transformations that usually lie behind them.

Surely it is no wonder. In what period have so many men been so totally exposed at so fast a pace to such earthquakes of change? That Americans have not known such catastrophic changes as have the men and women of other societies is due to historical facts that are now quickly becoming "merely history." The history that now affects every man is world history. Within this scene and this period, in the course of a single generation, one sixth of mankind is transformed from all that is feudal and backward into all that is modern, advanced, and fearful. Political colonies are freed; new and less visible forms of imperialism installed. Revolutions occur; men feel the intimate grip of new kinds of authority. Totalitarian societies rise, and are smashed to bits--or succeed fabulously. After two centuries of ascendancy, capitalism is shown up as only one way to make society into an industrial apparatus. After two centuries of hope, even formal democracy is restricted to a quite small portion of mankind. Everywhere in the underdeveloped world, ancient ways of life are broken up and vague expectations become urgent demands. Everywhere in the overdeveloped world, the means of authority and of violence become total in scope and bureaucratic in form. Humanity itself now lies before us, the super-nation at either pole concentrating its most coordinated and massive efforts upon the preparation of World War Three.

The very shaping of history now outpaces the ability of men to orient themselves in accordance with cherished values. And which values? Even when they do not panic, men often sense that older ways of feeling and thinking have collapsed and that newer beginnings are ambiguous to the point of moral stasis. Is it any wonder that ordinary men feel they cannot cope with the larger worlds with which they are so suddenly confronted? That they cannot understand the meaning of their epoch for their own lives? That--in defense of selfhood--they become morally insensible, trying to remain altogether private men? Is it any wonder that they come to be possessed by a sense of the trap?

It is not only information that they need--in this Age of Fact, information often dominates their attention and overwhelms their capacities to assimilate it. It is not only the skills of reason that they need--although their struggles to acquire these often exhaust their limited moral energy.

What they need, and what they feel they need, is a quality of mind that will help them to use information and to develop reason in order to achieve lucid summations of what is going on in the world and of what may be happening within themselves. It is this quality, I am going to contend, that journalists and scholars, artists and publics, scientists and editors, are coming to expect of what may be called the sociological imagination.

1.
The sociological imagination enables its possessor to understand the larger historical scene in terms of its meaning for the inner life and external career of a variety of individuals. It enables him to take into account how individuals, in the welter of their daily experience, often become falsely conscious of their social positions. Within that welter, the framework of modern society is sought, and within that framework the psychologies of a variety of men and women are formulated. By such means the personal uneasiness of individuals is focused upon explicit troubles and the indifference of publics is transformed into involvement with public issues.

The first fruit of this imagination--and the first lesson of the social science that embodies it--is the idea that the individual can understand his own experience and gauge his own fate only by locating himself within his period, that he can know his own chances in life only by becoming aware of those of all individuals in his circumstances. In many ways it is a terrible lesson; in many ways a magnificent one. We do not know the limits of man's capacities for supreme effort or willing degradation, for agony or glee, for pleasurable brutality or the sweetness of reason. But in our time we have come to know that the limits of "human nature" are frighteningly broad. We have come to know that every individual lives, from one generation to the next, in some society; that he lives out a biography, and that he lives it out within some historical sequence. By the fact of living he contributes, however minutely, to the shaping of this society and to the course of its history, even as he is made by society and bit its historical push and shove.

The sociological imagination enables us to grasp history and biography and the relations between the two within society. That is its task and its promise. To recognize this task and this promise is the mark of the classic social analyst. It is characteristic of Herbert Spencer--turgid, polysyllabic, comprehensive; of E. A. Ross--graceful, muckraking, upright; of Auguste Comte and Emile Durkheim; of the intricate and subtle Karl Mannheim. It is the quality of all that is intellectually excellent in Karl Marx; it is the clue to Thorstein Veblen's brilliant and ironic insight, to Joseph Schumpeter's many-sided constructions of reality; it is the basis of the psychological sweep of W. E. H. Lecky no less than of the profundity and clarity of Max Weber. And it is the signal of what is best in contemporary studies of man and society.

No social study that does not come back to the problems of biography, of history and of their intersections within a society has completed its intellectual journey. Whatever the specific problems of the classic social analysts, however limited or however broad the features of social reality they have examined, those who have been imaginatively aware of the promise of their work have consistently asked three sorts of questions:

(1) What is the structure of this particular society as a whole? What are its essential components, and how are they related to one another? How does it differ from other varieties of social order? Within it, what is the meaning of any particular feature for its continuance and for its change?

(2) Where does this society stand in human history? What are the mechanics by which it is changing? What is its place within and its meaning for the development of humanity as a whole? How does any particular feature we are examining affect, and how is it affected by, the historical period in which it moves? An this period--what are its essential features? How does it differ from other periods? What are its characteristic ways of history-making?

(3) What varieties of men and women now prevail in this society and in this period And what varieties are coming to prevail? In what ways are they selected and formed, liberated and repressed, made sensitive and blunted? What kinds of "human nature" are revealed in the conduct and character we observe in this society in this period? And what is the meaning for "human nature"; of each and every feature of the society we are examining?

Whether the point of interest is a great power state or a minor literary mood, a family, a prison, a creed--these are the kinds of questions that the best social analysts have asked. They are the intellectual pivots of classic studies of man in society--and they are the questions inevitably raised by any mind possessing the sociological imagination. For that imagination is the capacity to shift from one perspective to another--from the political to psychological; from examination of a single family to comparative assessment of the national budgets of the world; from the theological school to the military establishment; from considerations of an oil industry to studies of contemporary poetry. It is the capacity to range from the most impersonal and remote transformations to the most intimate features of the human self--and to see the relations between the two. Back of its use there is always the urge to know the social and historical meaning of the individual in the society and in the period in which he has his quality and his being.

That, in brief, is why it is by means of the sociological imagination that men now hope to grasp what is going on in the world, and to understand what is happening in themselves as minute points of the intersections of biography and history within society. In large part, contemporary man's self-realization of social relativity and of the transformative power of history. The sociological imagination is the most fruitful form of this self-consciousness. By its use men whose mentalities have swept only a series of limited orbits often come to feel as if suddenly awakened in a house with which they had only supposed themselves to be familiar. Correctly or incorrectly, they often come to feel that they can now provide themselves with adequate summations, cohesive assessments, comprehensive orientations. Older decisions that once appeared sound now seem to them products of a mind unaccountably dense. Their capacity for astonishment is made lively again. They acquire a new way of thinking, they experience a transvaluation of values: in a word, by their reflection and by their sensibility, they realize the cultural meaning of the social sciences.

2.
Perhaps the most fruitful distinction with which the sociological imagination works is between "the personal troubles of milieu" and "the public issues of social structure." This distinction is an essential tool of the sociological imagination and a feature of all classic work in social science.

Troubles occur within the character of the individual and within the range of his immediate relations with others; they have to do with his self and with those limited areas of social life of which he is directly and personally aware. Accordingly, the statement and the resolution of troubles properly lie within the individual as a biographical entity and within the scope of his immediate milieu--the social setting that is directly open to his personal experience and to some extent his willful activity. A trouble is a private matter: values cherished by an individual are felt by him to be threatened.

Issues have to do with matters that transcend these local environments of the individual and the range of his inner life. They have to do with the organization of many such milieux into the institutions of an historical society as a whole, with the ways in which various milieux overlap and interpenetrate to form the larger structure of social and historical life. An issue is a public matter:

some value cherished by publics is felt to be threatened. Often there is a debate about what that value really is and about what it is that really threatens it. This debate is often without focus if only because it is the very nature of an issue, unlike even widespread trouble, that it cannot very well be defined in terms of the immediate and everyday environments of ordinary men. An issue, in fact, often involves a crisis in institutional arrangements, and often too it involves what Marxists call "contradictions" or "antagonisms."

In these terms, consider unemployment. When, in a city of 100,000, only one man is unemployed, that is his personal trouble, and for its relief we properly look to the character of the man, his skills, and his immediate opportunities. But when in a nation of 50 million employees, 15 million men are unemployed, that is an issue, and we may not hope to find its solution within the range of opportunities open to any on individual. The very structure of opportunities has collapsed, both the correct statement of the problem and the range of possible solutions require us to consider the economic and political institutions of the society, and not merely the personal situation and character of a scatter of individuals.

Consider war. The personal problem of war, when it occurs, may be how to survive it or how to die in it with honor; how to make money out of it; how to climb into the higher safety of the military apparatus; or how to contribute to the war's termination. In short, according to one's values, to find a set of milieux and within it to survive the war or make one's death in it meaningful. But the structural issues of war have to do with its causes; with what types of men it throws up into command; with its effects upon economic and political, family, and religious institutions, with the unorganized irresponsibility of a world of nation-states.

Consider marriage. Inside a marriage a man and a woman may experience personal troubles, but when the divorce rate during the first four years of marriage is 250 out of every 1,000 attempts, this is an indication of a structural issue having to do with the institutions of marriage and the family and other institutions that bear upon them.

Or consider the metropolis--the horrible, beautiful, ugly, magnificent sprawl of the great city. For many upper-class people, the personal solution to "the problem of the city" is to have an apartment with private garage under it in the heart of the city, and forty miles out, a house by Henry Hill, garden by Garrett Eckbo, on a hundred acres of private land. In these two controlled environments-- with a small staff at each end and a private helicopter connection--most people could solve many of the problems of personal milieux cause by the facts of the city. But all this, however splendid, does not solve the public issues that the structural fact of the city poses. What should be done with this wonderful monstrosity? Break it all up into scattered units, combining residence and work? Refurbish it as it stands? Or, after evacuation, dynamite it and build new cities according to new plans in new places? What should those plans be? And who is to decide and to accomplish whatever choice is made? These are structural issues; to confront them and to solve them requires us to consider political and economic issues that affect innumerable milieux.

In so far as an economy is so arranged that slumps occur, the problem of unemployment becomes incapable of personal solution. In so far as war is inherent in the nation-state system and in the uneven industrialization of the world, the ordinary individual in his restricted milieu will be powerless--with or without psychiatric aid--to solve the troubles this system or lack of system imposes upon him. In so far as the family as an institution turns women into darling little slaves and men into their chief providers and unweaned dependents, the problem of a satisfactory marriage remains incapable of purely private solution. In so far as the overdeveloped megalopolis and the overdeveloped automobile are built--in features of the overdeveloped society, the issues of urban living will not be solved by personal ingenuity and private wealth.

What we experience in various and specific milieux, I have noted, is often caused by structural changes. Accordingly, to understand the changes of many personal milieux we are required to look beyond them. And the number and variety of such structural changes increase as the institutions within which we live become more embracing and more intricately connected with one another. To be aware of the idea of social structure and to use it with sensibility is to be capable of tracing such linkages among a great variety of milieux. To be able to do that is to possess the sociological imagination.■

1. From the reading, copy down one sentence that clarifies for you the meaning of the "sociological imagination."

2. Give three specific examples showing the link that exists between the life of the individual and what happens in the larger society (give examples relevant to today's society and preferably relating to you or to people you know).

3. Differentiate between "personal troubles of milieu" and the "public issues of social structure." Give two examples of each, beside those given in the text.

NOTES

CHAPTER 3

Culture

Objectives

This chapter introduces culture as the most important determinant of human behavior. Culture identifies a society, gives it its distinctive characteristics, sets it apart from other groups, and provides common grounds for people to interact with each other.

Here are some of the questions you may want to raise:

58 1. What are the components of culture and how is culture defined?

60 2. What is the role of culture and why the diversity of cultures? *learning is flexible*

3. Why is it that some groups of people within the same society exhibit different cultural characteristics? SAME AS #2

75 4. How do different groups within a society react to the same culture?

78 5. How do cultures develop and change over time?

Your own questions:

1) Culture consists of all beliefs, behaviors, and products common to the members of a particular group. Some components are: the values and customs that we hold in common with others; the language we speak; the rules we follow; the tools and technologies we use to make things; the goods that we make and consume; the organizations to which we belong; and the larger institutions to society.

3) One of sociology's central insights is that our lives and personalities are in large part ~~stained~~ constructed out of our shared culture

4) By assimilation, which is the process by which different cultures are absorbed into a single mainstream culture.

5) By cultural diffusion, which is the spread of one culture's characteristics to another culture

UNDERSTANDING YOUR OWN TEXTBOOK READING

1. Define the following:

   Pg. 58 culture: all of the beliefs, behaviors, and products common to the members of a particular group.

   Pg. 59 society: the interacting people who share a common culture

   pg 59 How can we study the origin and development of culture?
   through society

pg 60 2. Why is culture an important topic in sociology?
   culture is an important source of conformity.

pg 63 3. What is the difference between <u>material</u> culture and <u>non-material</u> culture? Give five examples of each (excluding those offered in the textbook).

   Material culture includes all the physical objects made by the members of a particular society to help shape their lives. Nonmaterial culture consists of all the nonphysical products of human interaction, that is, the ideas shared by people in a particular society.

pg 64 4. Name the major components (or elements) of non-material culture and give a brief description of each.

   language, values, beliefs, rules, institutions, and organizations

pg 69 5. Beside facilitating communication, what role does language play in culture?

   Language enables us to actively confer meaning on the world, and to derive meaning from it as well.

6. Define and give two examples of each:

sanctions: penalties for violations

norms: the shared rules in a particular culture that tell its members how to behave in a given situation

folkways: fairly weak norms that are passed down from the past, whose violation is generally not considered serious within a particular culture.

mores: strongly held norms whose violation would seriously offend the standards of acceptable conduct of most people within a particular culture.

laws: codified norms or rules of behavior that have been officially legislated by a governing body and are backed by the use of force.

7. Distinguish between <u>folkways</u>, <u>mores</u>, and <u>laws</u>, giving examples of each that deal with the same type of behavior (for example, the way people dress, eat, drive, etc.).

folkways - Students should be reasonably dressed in college, but some wear cut-off T-shirts.

Mores - a university student who removed all clothing before class

laws - a local ordinance outlawing nudity in public places

8. Explain and give examples of <u>cultural lag</u> and <u>cultural diffusion</u> in our society.

Cultural lag is a tendency for different parts of the nonmaterial culture to change at different rates in response to technological innovations or other sources of change in the material culture. Cultural diffusion is the spread of one culture's characteristics to another culture.

9. Define subcultures. Identify a subculture in American society and indicate its functions and dysfunctions.

Subculture is a smaller culture that exists within a larger, dominate culture yet differs from it in some important way.

pg 75 10. Give two examples of countercultures in American society. How are they different from subcultures?

The hippies of the 1960's, "Deadheads"
The difference between the two is that the counterculture developed in self-conscious opposition to the prevailing culture which it hoped to influence through its oppositional lifestyle

pg 76 11. Define ethnocentrism and cultural relativism. What can be seen as positive and negative aspects of each?

Ethnocentrism is the tendency to judge other cultures by the standards of one's own culture. Culture relativism is the attitude that the practices of another society should be understood sociologically in terms of that society's own norms and values, and not one's own.

pg 79 12. How can we talk of a universal culture in the modern world? What factors encourage the development of such a trend?

Although people may move around the world, they frequently continue to identify with their culture of origin.

TESTING YOUR KNOWLEDGE

True and False

1. Culture can be observed only in highly developed societies. — T **F**

2. Some societies have only material culture, while some others have only non-material culture. — T **F**

3. Norms are based on values. — **T** F

4. Since each society has its own distinct culture, there are no common elements to their social structures. — T **F**

5. Norms and sanctions are aspects of the material culture. — T **F**

6. Cultural universals are practices found in every culture. — **T** F

7. "Subculture" is another word for "counterculture." — T **F**

8. ~~Sanctions are always negative, while norms are always positive.~~ — T F

9. ~~Cultural integration is the acceptance of all norms by all members of a society.~~ — T F

10. Ethnocentrism is the opposite of cultural relativism. — **T** F

11. ~~Popular songs and children's games can contribute to cultural integration.~~ — T F

12. People no longer identify strongly with their cultures of origin. — T **F**

Multiple Choice

1. A fairly large group of people organized under a given ~~political authority~~ *shared cultural norms* and occupying a common geographic area is known as a: _____

   a. political institution
   (b) society
   c. formal organization
   d. culture

2. The sum of socially transmitted beliefs, norms, and behaviors constitutes: _____

   a. a society
   b. a subculture
   (c) a culture
   d. an ecosystem

3. Sociologists make a distinction between two aspects of culture: _____

   a. real and ideal
   b. material and spiritual
   c. general and specific
   (d) material and non-material

4. Chopsticks, forks, spoons, and knives are examples of: _____

   (a) material culture
   b. irrelevant culture
   c. normative culture
   d. practical culture

5. Commonly shared knowledge, beliefs, values, and norms are examples of: _____

   a. material culture
   b. spiritual culture
   c. significant culture
   (d) none of the above

6. Practices such as language, courtship, and bodily adornment, are examples of: _____

   (a) cultural universals
   b. cultural diffusion
   c. cultural integration
   d. cultural variations

7. Cultural variations can result in: _____

   (a) subcultures
   b. countercultures
   c. culture shock
   d. all of the above

34

8. Socially defined expectations of behavior are called: _____
    a. subculture
    b. moral code of ethics
    c. ideologies
    d. norms

9. The concept of multiculturalism is best represented by the image of: _____
    a. "the melting pot"
    b. "the salad bowl"
    c. "the boiling pot"
    d. "the marching band"

10. Ethnocentrism can be seen as: _____
    a. both functional and dysfunctional
    b. always dysfunctional
    c. always functional
    d. serving the interests of the dominant group only

ESSAY PRACTICE

pg 691. Define the "Sapir-Whorf Hypothesis," also known as the "linguistic relativity hypothesis." Give some examples that would apply to our society.

Perceptions are relative to language. Does not hold that language determines perception, only that one is most likely to attend to differences for which one has a word or a concept.

pg 692. List as many words as you can think of to express <u>money</u> in the American language. What does that say about our society?

cash
bucks
dinero
cake

CRITICAL THINKING EXERCISES

1. Write down your own concept of the "American dream." What values would underlie your views? How does your description reflect the American culture?

2. Discuss two of the recent changes in American values and beliefs. How do they affect today's college generation. Do you foresee any more changes in the near future (affecting, perhaps, the next generation)?

ADDITIONAL READING AND SPECIAL PROJECT

Bring to class a short report or some notes on a fiction, short story, poetry, song, or other literary piece depicting aspects of the American culture. Be prepared to share your findings with your classmates, and discuss specifics, such as norms, practices, customs, values, behaviors, etc., evidenced in your chosen piece. You may also select literature showing aspects of a different culture.

A WORLD VIEW OF CULTURAL DIVERSITY
Thomas Sowell

Diversity has become one of the most often used words of our time--and a word almost never defined. Diversity is invoked in discussions of everything from employment policy to curriculum reform and from entertainment to politics. Nor is the word merely a description of the long-known fact that the American population is made up of people from many countries, many races, and many cultural backgrounds. All this was well known long before the word "diversity" became an insistent part of our vocabulary, an invocation, an imperative, or a bludgeon in ideological conflicts.

The very motto of the country, *E Pluribus Unum*, recognizes the diversity of the American people. For generations, this diversity has been celebrated, whether in comedies like *Abie's Irish Rose* (the famous play featuring a Jewish boy and an Irish girl) or in patriotic speeches on the Fourth of July. Yet one senses something very different in celebration of America and often a sweeping criticism of the United States, or even a condemnation of Western civilization as a whole.

At the very least, we need to separate the issue of the general importance of cultural diversity--not only in the United States but in the world at large--from the more specific, more parochial, and more ideological agendas that have become associated with this word in recent years. I would like to talk about the worldwide importance of cultural diversity over centuries of human history before returning to the narrower issues of our time.

The entire history of the human race, the rise of man from the caves, has been marked by transfers of cultural advances from one group to another and from one civilization to another. Paper and printing, for example, are today vital parts of Western civilization, but they originated in China centuries before they made their way to Europe. So did the magnetic compass, which made possible the great ages of exploration that put the Western hemisphere in touch with the rest of mankind. Mathematical concepts likewise migrated from one culture to another: trigonometry from ancient Egypt, and the whole numbering system now used throughout the world originated among the Hindus of India, though Europeans called this system Arabic numerals because it was the Arabs who were the intermediaries through which these numbers reached medieval Europe. Indeed, much of the philosophy of ancient Greece first reached Western Europe in Arabic translations, which were then retranslated into Latin or into the vernacular languages of the West Europeans.

Much that became part of the culture of Western civilization originated outside that civilization, often in the Middle East or Asia. The later rise of Western Europe to world preeminence in science and technology built upon these foundations, and then the science and technology of European civilization began to spread around the world, not only to European offshoot societies such as the United States or Australia, but also to non-European cultures, of which Japan is perhaps the most striking example.

The historic sharing of cultural advances, until they became the common inheritance of the human race, implied much more than cultural diversity. It implied that some cultural features were not only different from others but better than others. The very fact that people--all people, whether Europeans, Africans, Asians, or others--have repeatedly chosen to abandon some feature of their own culture in order to replace it with something from another culture implies that the replacement served their purposes more effectively. Arabic numerals are not simply different from Roman numeral, they are better than Roman numerals. This is shown by their replacing Roman numerals in many countries whose cultures derived from Rome, as well as in other countries who respective numbering systems were likewise superseded by so-called Arabic numerals. Clearly, cultural leadership in various fields has changed hands many times. China was far in advance of any country in Europe in a large number of fields for at least a thousand years and, as late as the sixteenth century, had the highest standard of living in the world. Equally clearly, China today is one of the poorer nations of the world and is having great difficulty trying to catch up to the technological level of Japan and the West, with no real hope of regaining its former world preeminence in the foreseeable future.

Just as cultural leadership in a particular field is not permanent for nations or civilizations, neither is it permanent for given racial, ethnic, or religious groups. By the time the Jews were expelled from Spain in 1492, Europe had overtaken the Islamic world in medical science, so that Jewish physicians who sought refuge in the Ottoman Empire found themselves in great demand in that Moslem country. By the early sixteenth century, the sultan of the Ottoman Empire had on his palace medical staff forty-two Jewish physicians and twenty-one Moslem physicians.

What are the implications of a world view of cultural diversity on the narrower issues being debated under that label in the United States today? Although "diversity" is used in so many different ways in so many different contexts that it seems to mean all things to all people, there are a few themes that appear again and again. One of these broad themes is that diversity implies organized efforts at the preservation of cultural differences, perhaps governmental efforts, perhaps government subsidies to various programs run by the advocates of diversity.

This approach raises questions as to what the purpose of culture is. If what is important about cultures is that they are emotionally symbolic, and if differentness is cherished for the sake of differentness, then this particular version of cultural diversity might make some sense. But cultures exist even in isolated societies where there are not other cultures around--where there is no one else and nothing else from which to be different. Cultures exist to serve the vital, practical requirements of human life--to structure a society so as to perpetuate the species, to pass on the hard-earned knowledge and experience of generations past and centuries past to the young and inexperienced in order to spare the next generation the costly and dangerous process of learning everything all over again from scratch through trial and error--including fatal errors. Cultures exist so that people can know how to get food and put a roof over their heads, how to cure the sick, how to cope with the death of the loved ones, and how to get along with the living. Cultures are not bumper stickers. They are living, changing ways of doing all the things that have to be done in life.

Every culture discards over time the things that no longer do the job or which do not do the job as well as things borrowed from other cultures. Each individual does this consciously or not, on a day-to-day basis. Languages take words from other languages, so that Spanish as spoken in Argentina has Italian words taken from the large Italian immigrant population there. This in not what some of the advocates of diversity have in mind. They seem to want to preserve cultures in their purity, almost like butterflies preserved in amber. Decisions about change, if any, seem to be regarded as collective decisions, political decisions. But this is not how cultures have arrived where they are. Individuals have decided for themselves how much of the old they wished to retain, how much of the new they found useful in their own lives.

In this way, cultures have enriched each other in all the great civilizations of the world. In this way, great port cities and other crossroads of cultures have become centers of progress all across the planet. No culture has grown great in isolation--but a number of cultures have made historic and even astonishing advances when their isolations was ended, usually by events beyond their control.

We need also to recognize that many great thinkers of the past labored not simply to advance whatever particular group they happened to have come from but to advance the human race. Their legacies, whether cures for deadly diseases or dramatic increases in crop yields to fight the scourge of hunger, belong to all people--and all people need to claim that legacy, not seal themselves off in a dead end of tribalism or in an emotional orgy of cultural vanity.■

NOTES

NOTES

CHAPTER 4

Societies and Social Structure

Objectives

Each society has its own pattern of social interaction that reflects its particular culture. The social structure provides a framework for predictable human behaviors. It is also the immediate context within which day to day interactions usually occur.

Here are some of the questions you may want to raise:

1. How is social structure defined and what role does it play in social interactions?

2. What are the components of the social structure and how do they relate to individuals and groups?

3. Does the social structure of a given society change over time?

4. What is the relationship between culture and social structure?

Your own questions:

UNDERSTANDING YOUR OWN TEXTBOOK READING

1. A social structure can be defined as:

2. Name five social structures you are familiar with:

3. Name and briefly explain the elements of social structure:

4. Fill in the diagram below by listing ten each of <u>your own</u> ascribed and achieved statuses.

Your Name:

ASCRIBED STATUSES		ACHIEVED STATUSES
_____		_____
_____	**MASTER STATUS:**	_____
_____	_____	_____
_____		_____
_____		_____
_____		_____
_____		_____
_____		_____
_____		_____

5. Pick one of the statuses listed on the previous question. List five roles related to that particular status.

6. Define social institution and give two examples of social institutions.

7. Describe the major features of "hunting and gathering societies."

8. What made it possible for settlements to emerge in pastoral societies?

9. What differentiates agricultural from horticultural societies?

10. What are some major characteristics of the industrial society?

11. What are the contradictions of the industrial society?

12. Summarize the characteristics of post-industrial societies.

TESTING YOUR KNOWLEDGE

True and False

1. Society can be viewed as being made up of a set of social positions. T F

2. A master status is a position of dominance one occupies, such as president of a company. T F

3. Institutions are forms of organization that perform basic functions in a society. T F

4. Our response to someone's behavior is based on our interpretation of what the behavior means. T F

5. The term <u>industrial revolution</u> refers to the period beginning with the 20th century. T F

6. Important social statuses have no roles attached to them. T F

7. Role ambiguity may lead to role strain. T F

8. Role conflicts pose no ethical choices: they are resolved by prescribed social norms. T F

9. Social groups are an element of social structure. T F

10. Feudalism is a form of stratification associated with agricultural societies. T F

11. A social network is set of relationships among close friends. T F

12. Knowledge, information, and services are important features of the post-industrial society. T F

Multiple Choice

1. Social structure is concerned with: _____

    a. the organization of society
    b. social positions within the society
    c. the distribution of resources within the society
    d. all of the above

2. Interacting people who share a common culture can be called: _____

    a. a structural contradiction
    b. a society
    c. a role conflict
    d. an example of globalization

3. A position within a social structure is called: _____

    a. a status
    b. a role
    c. a norm
    d. a symbol

4. A status which is assigned to a person, generally at birth, without taking into account the person's choice or merit, is defined as: _____

    a. ascribed
    b. achieved
    c. arbitrary
    d. master

5. An expectation of behavior within a given status is called: _____

    a. social role
    b. social constraint
    c. social stratification
    d. master status

6. When people are unclear about what is expected of them in a given situation, they are likely to experience: _____

    a. role conflict
    b. role ambiguity
    c. role exit
    d. none of the above

48

7. Which of the following is not an example of social institutions? _____

   a. the government
   b. the mass media
   c. a birthday party
   d. the health care system

8. Which of the following is not a feature of the industrial society? _____

   a. work is increasingly centered in factories
   b. the home is the primary unit of production
   c. there is an enormous increase in bureaucracy
   d. governments become more powerful

9. The production of surplus was first made possible with: _____

   a. hunting and gathering societies
   b. pastoral societies
   c. horticultural societies
   d. industrial societies

10. Sociologist Ferdinand Tonnies uses this term to describe the kind of relationship that characterizes a close-knit community: _____

    a. Gemeinschaft
    b. Gesellschaft
    c. Verstehen
    d. communal solidarity

ESSAY PRACTICE

1. Establish the difference between role ambiguity, role strain, and role conflict. Then provide an example of each as it has applied to you. How did you deal with the situation?

2. Summarize the conflict and interactionist views of social institutions.

CRITICAL THINKING EXERCISES

1. Compare the quality of life in industrial and post-industrial societies.

2. What do sociologists mean by definition and construction of reality? What do you think of the concept? How does it apply to our everyday life?

NOTES

CHAPTER 5

Socialization

Objectives

The process of learning how to become a functional member of our society is the topic of this chapter. Through a lifelong process of interaction, people internalize social norms, values, beliefs, and attitudes which enable them to relate to their society, while giving them their unique personality. Various learning theories and the principal agents of socialization are discussed in this chapter.

Here are some of the questions you may want to raise:

1. What is socialization and how does it shape people's behavior and personality?

2. What part do our inherited characteristics play in the socialization process?

3. Which one plays a greater role in shaping our personality: our genetic disposition or our social environment?

4. Are we entirely controlled by society or do we have a free will?

5. What are the major theories of socialization?

6. How do the socialization agents shape our thinking and behavior? Are some more important than others?

Your own questions:

UNDERSTANDING YOUR OWN TEXTBOOK READING

1. Socialization is the process whereby:

2. Through this process, people learn _____, _____, and they develop a _____.

3. The term <u>nature</u> refers to _____, whereby <u>nurture</u> refers to _____.

4. What roles do nature and nurture play in shaping our unique personality?

5. Mead refers to the period of early childhood as _____ _____.

6. Define the following:

   significant others:

   generalized others:

   role models:

   In which one of Mead's stages is each one of these most significant?

7. The theory of the looking-glass self was developed by _____.

8. Name the social scientists who have built their socialization theories around <u>stages</u>.

9. Briefly describe Kohlberg's stages of moral development.

10. Define and give examples of:

   rites of passage:

   anticipatory socialization:

   resocialization:

   total institutions:

TESTING YOUR KNOWLEDGE

True and False

1. Children deprived of early human interaction experience no lasting developmental and emotional problems. T F

2. The self-image develops as a result of human interaction. T F

3. For most people, moral behavior is conditioned by rewards and punishments. T F

4. The sociopath has an overdeveloped conscience. T F

5. According to Erikson's eight stages of life, children who get excessively negative messages tend to adapt well to society and be highly motivated to achieve. T F

6. Erikson gives a greater role to nurture in defining the dilemmas to be resolved at various stages of life. T F

7. Socialization is usually completed by early adulthood. T F

8. Self-concept has no influence on behavior: it is only an attitude. T F

9. Resocialization occurs in total institutions. T F

10. Conflicting pressures from important people in our lives rarely lead to stress for the individual. T F

11. Nature and nurture are mutually exclusive in the socialization process. T F

12. Sociobiology reflects the view of the conflict perspective. T F

Multiple Choice

1. One of the first sociologists to examine the socialization process from the interactionist perspective is: _____

    a. Margaret Mead
    b. Charles Horton Cooley
    c. George Herbert Mead
    d. Sigmund Freud

2. According to Mead's theory, which is the source of the spontaneous and seemingly unpredictable side of a person's behavior? _____

    a. the "I"
    b. the "me"
    c. the significant other
    d. the role model

3. According to Freud, the conscience that arises from messages we get from others concerning what is and is not acceptable behavior is called: _____

    a. the id
    b. the superego
    c. the alter ego
    d. the deflated self

4. Bobbie obeys the speed limit on the freeway only when he knows that there is a traffic patrol car in the area. According to Kohlberg, Bobbie is functioning at what level of moral development? _____

    a. conventional
    b. pre-conventional
    c. unconventional
    d. post conventional

5. The process whereby new members of a society learn how to behave and develop their self-concepts is: _____

    a. formal education
    b. cultural patterning
    c. socialization
    d. total socialization

6. Specific individuals with whom a person interacts and who are important in a person's life are: _____

    a. social modes
    b. generalized others
    c. significant others
    d. important others

7. According to George H. Mead, role taking is an important aspect of the: _____

   a. game stage
   b. sport stage
   c. generalized others stage
   d. play stage

8. At this stage, the child can consider taking on several roles simultaneously: _____

   a. play stage
   b. game stage
   c. imitation stage
   d. conventional stage

9. In Freudian theory, the self is a social product that results from the interaction and conflict between: _____

   a. our drives for fun and gratification
   b. our inner instincts and the constraints imposed by society
   c. our religious beliefs and social laws
   d. personal ethics and religious values

10. Cognitive development theories focus on: _____

    a. mental processes of learning
    b. stages of learning
    c. both a and b
    d. none of the above

11. The stages of socialization do not include which of the following? _____

    a. socially shared view of appropriate age range for major life events
    b. a series of plateaus reached in the socialization process
    c. learning the behavior appropriate to each new social role
    d. anticipatory socialization

12. The most important agent of socialization for children in the U.S. is: _____

    a. the school
    b. the family
    c. the peer group
    d. the church

13. Parents changing their thinking of behavior patterns as a result of their interaction with their children is an example of: _____

    a. reverse socialization
    b. total socialization
    c. cultural integration
    d. identity exchange

14. The dramaturgical approach was developed by: _____
    a. Sigmund Freud
    b. Lawrence Kohlberg
    c. Irving Goffman
    d. Daniel Levinson

ESSAY PRACTICE

Summarize each of the agents of socialization described in your textbook, indicating the overall influence of each at different stages of your life.

CRITICAL THINKING EXERCISES

Could we explain the increase in juvenile delinquency by the large number of conflicting messages in the socialization process? Give examples.

MY DAUGHTER SMOKES
Alice Walker

My daughter smokes. While she is doing her homework, her feet on the bench in front of her and her calculator clicking out answers to her algebra problems, I am looking at the half-empty package of Camels tossed carelessly close at hand. Camels. I pick them up, take them into the kitchen, where the light is better, and study them--they're filtered, for which I am grateful. My heart feels terrible. I want to weep. In fact, I do weep a little, standing there by the stove holding one of the instruments, so white, so precisely rolled, that could cause my daughter's death. When she smoked Marlboros and Players I hardened myself against feeling so bad; nobody I knew ever smoked these brands.

She doesn't know this, but it was Camels that my father, her grandfather, smoked. But before he smoked "ready-mades"--when he was very young and very poor, with eyes like lanterns--he smoked Prince Albert tobacco in cigarettes he rolled himself. I remember the bright-red tobacco tin, with a picture of Queen Victoria's consort, Prince Albert, dressed in a black frock coat and carrying a cane.

The tobacco was dark brown, pungent, slightly bitter. I tasted it more than once as a child, and the discarded tins could be used for a number of things: to keep buttons and shoelaces in, to store seeds, and best of all, to hold worms for the rare times my father took us fishing.

By the late forties and early fifties no one rolled his own anymore (and few women smoked) in my hometown, Eatonton, Georgia. The tobacco industry, coupled with Hollywood movies in which both hero and heroine smoked like chimneys, won over completely people like my father, who were hopelessly addicted to cigarettes. He never looked as dapper as Prince Albert, though; he continued to look like a poor overweight, overworked colored man with too large a family; black, with a very white cigarette stuck in his mouth.

I do not remember when he started to cough. Perhaps it was unnoticeable at first. A little hacking in the morning as he lit his first cigarette upon getting out of bed. By the time I was my daughter's age, he breath was a wheeze, embarrassing to hear; he could not climb stairs without resting every third or fourth step. It was not unusual for him to cough for an hour.

It is hard to believe there was a time when people did not understand that cigarette smoking is an addiction. I wondered aloud once to my sister--who is perennially trying to quit--whether our father realized this. I wondered how she, a smoker since high school, viewed her own habit.

It was our father who gave her first cigarette, one day when she had taken water to him in the fields.

"I always wondered why he did that," she said, puzzled and with some bitterness.

"What did he say?" I asked.

"That he didn't want me to go to anyone else for them," she said, "which never really crossed my mind."

So he was aware it was addictive, I thought, though as annoyed as she that he assumed she would be interested.

I began smoking in eleventh grade, also the year I drank numerous bottles of terrible sweet, very cheap wine. My friends and I, all boys for this venture, bought our supplies from a man who ran a segregated bar and liquor store on the outskirts of town. Over the entrance there was a large sign that said COLORED. We were not permitted to drink there, only to buy. I smoked Kools, because my sister did. By then I thought her toxic darkened lips and gums glamorous. However, my body simply would not tolerate smoke. After six months, I had a chronic sore throat. I gave up smoking, gladly. Because it was a ritual with my buddies--Murl, Leon, and "Dog" Farley--I continued to drink wine.

My father died from "the poor man's friend," pneumonia, one hard winter when his bronchitis and emphysema had left him low. I doubt he had much lung left at all, after coughing for so many years. He had so little breath that, during his last years, he was always leaning on something. I remember once, at a family reunion, when my daughter was two, that my father picked her up for a minute-- long enough for me to photograph them--but the effort was obvious. Near the very end of his life, and largely because he had no more lungs, he quit smoking. He gained a couple of pounds, but by then he was so emaciated no one noticed.

When I travel to Third World countries I see many people like my father and daughter. There are large billboards directed at them both: the tough, "take-charge," or dapper older man, the glamorous, "worldly" young woman, both puffing away. In these poor countries, as in American ghettos and on reservations, money that should be spent for food goes instead to the tobacco companies; over time, people starve themselves of both food and air, effectively weakening and addicting their children, eventually eradicating themselves. I read in the newspaper and in my gardening magazine that cigarette butts are so toxic that if a baby swallows one, it is likely to die, and that the boiled water from a bunch of them makes an effective insecticide.

My daughter would like to quit, she says. We both know the statistics are against her; most people who try to quit smoking do not succeed.

There is a deep hurt that I feel as a mother. Some days it is a feeling of futility. I remember how carefully I ate when I was pregnant, how patiently I taught my daughter how to cross a street safely. For what, I sometimes wonder; so that she can wheeze through most of her life feeling half her strength, and then die of self-poisoning, as her grandfather did?

But, finally, one must feel empathy for the tobacco plant itself. For thousands of years, it has been venerated by Native Americans as a sacred medicine. They have used it extensively--its juice, its leaves, its roots, its (holy) smoke--to heal wounds and cure diseases, and in ceremonies of prayer and peace. And though the plant as most of us know it has been poisoned by chemicals denatured by intensive mono-cropping and is therefore hardly the plant it was, still, to some modern Indians it remains a plant of positive power. I learned this when my Native American friends, Bill Wahpepah and his family, visited with me for a few days and the first thing he did was sow a few tobacco seeds in my garden.

Perhaps we can liberate tobacco from those who have captured and abused it, enslaving the plant on large plantations, keeping it from freedom and its kin, and forcing it to enslave the world. Its true nature suppressed, no wonder it has become deadly. Maybe by sowing a few seeds of tobacco in our gardens and treating the plant with the reverence it deserves, we can redeem tobacco's soul and restore its self-respect.

Besides, how grim, if one is a smoker, to realize one is smoking a slave.

There is a slogan from a battered women's shelter that I especially like: "Peace on earth begins as home." I believe everything does. I think of a slogan for people trying to stop smoking: "Every home a smoke-free zone." Smoking is a form of self-battering that also batters those who must sit by, occasionally cajole or complain, and helplessly watch. I realize now that as a child I sat by, through the years, and literally watched my father kill himself: surely one such victory in my family, for the rich white men who own the tobacco companies, is enough. ■

NOTES

NOTES

CHAPTER 6

Groups and Organizations

Objectives

Through this chapter, you will familiarize yourself with the structure and dynamics of groups and social organizations, particularly formal organizations. You will learn about the functions and dysfunctions of groups and formal organizations, and analyze bureaucracy within the theoretical framework of major social scientists.

Here are some of the questions you may want to raise:

1. What is the difference between groups and organizations?

2. Are there different types of groups, and if so, what are they?

3. What difference does the size of the group make?

4. Is group work better than individual work?

5. How can groups function at their peak efficiency?

6. What makes a group work well? What makes it dysfunctional?

7. What are the characteristics of an effective group leader? What makes a group leader inefficient?

8. How come bureaucracies are usually so frustrating to deal with? How can they respond better to people's needs?

Your own questions:

UNDERSTANDING YOUR OWN TEXTBOOK READING

1. Write the definition of <u>social group</u> given in your textbook. Number and underline the several different significant components of this definition. How many did you find?

2. Rewrite the definition in several, but complete, sentences (at least three), using your own words.

3. Repeat the same exercise for the definition of <u>formal organization</u>.

4. The smallest possible group is called a _____ and is made of _____ people. A triad is composed of _____ people.

5. Define the following and give examples of each:

   primary group:

   secondary group:

   reference group:

6. List three of your own <u>ingroups</u> and three of your <u>outgroups</u>. What is the difference between the two?

7. List three characteristics shared by all formal organizations:

8. Compare the "scientific management" approach to the "human relations" approach in bureaucratic organization.

9. Give several reasons why people belong to voluntary associations.

10. List and briefly summarize the dysfunctions of bureaucracy. Which ones have you experienced more often? Which one do you think is the most frustrating?

11. Why are informal structures created in formal organizations?

12. What two lessons can be derived from the Zimbardo prison experiment?

13. List the new trends in work organization exemplified by the Japanese system.

14. Name the sociologists who have significantly contributed to our understanding of formal organization. Briefly summarize their respective contributions.

TESTING YOUR KNOWLEDGE

True and False

1. The term "social group" is used to refer to more than two people. T F

2. The dynamics of groups are the same regardless of the group size. T F

3. Larger groups tend to be more stable than smaller ones. T F

4. Secondary groups are always large groups. T F

5. The importance of primary groups has been displaced by that of secondary groups in post-industrial societies. T F

6. Because of ethnocentrism, an outgroup that does things differently will often be seen as inferior. T F

7. Outside threats generally tend to favor group cohesion. T F

8. Formal organizations usually have the same purposes. T F

9. Coalitions can develop in a dyad. T F

10. The symbolic interactionist perspective focuses on the formal structure of bureaucracies. T F

Multiple Choice

1. Family, roommates, and close friends are examples of: _____
    a. primary group
    b. secondary group
    c. outgroup
    d. instrumental group

2. The term <u>dyad</u> means: _____
    a. a dialogue between two people
    b. an argument about conflicting views
    c. a group of two people
    d. none of the above

3. Which of the following is a voluntary organization? _____
    a. a prison
    b. a mental institution
    c. the YMCA
    d. all of the above

4. Which of the following is a coercive organization? _____
    a. a prison
    b. a self-help group
    c. a church
    d. a labor union

5. A social group a person does not belong to, or does not identify with, is called: _____
    a. a gang
    b. an outgroup
    c. a kinship group
    d. an outsider's group

6. Which of the following represents Michel's principle that in an organization, power tends to be concentrated in the hands of leaders who use that power to foster their own interests? _____
    a. the iron law of oligarchy
    b. the iron law of governance
    c. management by objectives
    d. none of the above

7. A leader whose power comes from the leader's own personality is said to exercise: _____

   a. authority
   b. power
   c. personal power
   d. positional power

8. _____ developed an ideal type of bureaucracy and was the first sociologist to examine in detail the characteristics of bureaucracy.

   a. George Simmel
   b. Karl Marx
   c. Max Weber
   d. Margaret Murray Washington

9. People generally use these groups as standards when evaluating themselves: _____

   a. reference groups
   b. comparison groups
   c. interaction process groups
   d. modeling groups

10. Research on work productivity consistently finds that, when workers are given more control over their work situation, the following usually occurs: _____

    a. productivity increases
    b. productivity decreases
    c. company waste increases
    d. workers' morale decreases

11. According to Weber, the process by which business decisions are made on the basis of what is expected to work best: _____

    a. informal structure
    b. groupthink
    c. rationalization
    d. expressive bureaucracy

12. The management technique known as "quality circles" originated in: _____

    a. The United States
    b. Japan
    c. Sweden
    d. Germany

ESSAY PRACTICE

1. Briefly summarize the positive aspects of bureaucracies.

2. Write your assessment of Milgram's experiment. Do you think it would lead to the same conclusions today? Why?

CRITICAL THINKING EXERCISES

1. Debate Michel's and Weber's views of bureaucracy. How do they relate to the functioning of democracy?

2. Carefully review the trends in work organization offered by the Japanese model. How can it be adapted to American management?

SLIM'S TABLE
Mitchell Duneier

For the black regulars, passing time at Valois (cafeteria) consists of participating in the same rhythm of various routinized episodes that yield both companionship and solitude. These repetitive sequences are significant because they guarantee the recurrent presence of close acquaintances while establishing them as people who have "things to do." The routines of most of the men therefore demonstrate full awareness of the times when they might be in the way at the cafeteria. Rather than put themselves in the position of spending too much time in one place, they make a point of developing routines that show a certain independence of the establishment. No matter how gratifying collective life can be, excessive time spent in one place can demean a man. This is why routines also function to guard the individual against a likely challenge to his pride. Self-respecting people cannot help experiencing a certain amount of embarrassment when they appear to others to have nothing to do and no place to go. As Luther, a newsstand attendant, says: "A man without things to do is not a man."

Clearly defined personal activities and repetitive processes are constituents of both individual autonomy and collective solidarity. Collective life among the black regulars is therefore characterized by intermittence and recurrence. The same people are usually present at similar times each day or week. But gatherings do not necessarily occur among them with that same regularity. Collective life does not consist of a continuous flow of interactions among all the members. It is, rather, a now-and-then phenomenon that occurs with some unpredictability, in varying arrangements, from day to day. A few habitués routinely sit alone at separate tables and only join members of the larger collectivity on rare occasions; many choose to sit by themselves at least sometimes. Most participate in a variety of subgroups drawn from the wider collectivity of black men.

It is not uncommon for individuals to begin by sitting with a small group, later to change partners or move to another table by themselves. Often men who gather at one table will engage in constant conversation; at other times those same men will sit quietly with one another or simply make occasional comments while reading their newspapers in each other's presence. The average length of these gatherings is about forty-five minutes but it is not unusual for men to sit together for twice that length of time.

Some of the black cafeteria regulars are retired, others still work. Hanging out, not unlike traditional forms of work, is organized around specific bundles of tasks that need to be accomplished if only to satisfy obligations to oneself. The example of Drake is illustrative. He is a retired butcher who brings lottery tickets to the Greek owners every night in exchange for reimbursement and a cup of tea with lemon. He sometimes works as a substitute at the newsstand on the same block as the restaurant. Seven days a week he travels on the but from his nursing home, eight blocks away in the ghetto, to Fifty-third street. Men like Drake create satisfactions for themselves by establishing, in their times of leisure, conditions not unlike those of their former jobs.

Hanging out consists of discovering types of activity that result in predictable and desired amounts of companionship, conviviality, and solitude, and the ability to bring about new experiences by changing the conditions within each type of activity. Contrasts and choices among the alternatives are made manifest after men have been inside the cafeteria for an extended period of time. It is common for them to alter the conditions of passing time by joining new people at other tables or even by moving away from a group to sit alone for a period of time. The social world is large enough--especially when the cafeteria is crowded--to ensure that each man can sit with many others without ever getting tired of their company. It is through such processes that men with time on their hands avoid boredom.

There are middle-class people in the Hyde Parke neighborhood who view the black men at Valois as bums and loafers. But the men involved--like Drake--experience their days as productive. They have been molded by ideals and necessities of the conditions of their work. The black regulars seem to be temperamentally suited to establishing routines that provide maximum satisfaction from simply keeping busy, engaging in a range of repetitious activities from day to day. This enables them to preserve their self-esteem and to feel they are taking part in chosen activities, rather than residual ones, and this in turn helps them to feel that their own lives are meaningful.

Although the men often congregate at the same table, it is not unusual for them to settle in separately, without even acknowledging the presence of those with whom they sat only a day or a meal earlier. Normally they mingle with the same general group of sitting buddies, but not always. Sometimes the same men might sit together no more than once every few weeks. But regardless of the extent to which collective life is intermittent, individuals do tend to be present on the same schedules each day. There is always a balance between copresence and intermittence.

Regardless of the extent to which collective life takes on a now-and-then character, such rhythmic sequences bring about the recurrent presence of the same group of others in a man's life. Although interaction is frequently interrupted, the routines of those involved are nevertheless important to the group. They are the vehicle by which the black men can depend upon the recurrent presence of specific others in their lives.

If a man is asked why he hangs out with the same people at the same times throughout the year, he may say, as one man did to me, that it is just happenstance or he may deny the existence of repetitive sequences altogether, so as not to imply they he is a creature of habit. But if some do not recognize or admit to their own routines, they are the exception rather than the rule. In fact, the very significance of routines to collective life is sometimes a topic of discussion among the men themselves. They also show specific awareness of the time patterns of each of their companions. The image of collective life in the minds of group members is partly a function of each man's awareness of the routines of his associates. The sense that one is a member of a collective life is served by knowledge that he participates in a common repetitive process.

A man places a value on his own recurrent patterns and on those of his friends as well. This is the case not only for those with whom he sits frequently but also for persons he encounters at more unpredictable intervals. Comments and questions like, "You're late tonight" or "Why have you been late the last few nights?" or "Where have you been? We were worried about you!" were heard over and over again. Whether explicitly stated or not, one reason many men come to the cafeteria at particular times is that they are expected--and they come to expect others to be there as well. Particular routines are a vehicle by which both self-respect and companionship with the same people are maintained. The expectation of regular participation in collective life is one of the greatest single sources of support a man can find--short of a wife and children.

The disposition to be honest rather than to create fictions that might serve to prop up others' sense of one's own value is the true achievement of worth in the eyes of their associates. By living in accordance with principles such as pride, civility, sincerity, and discretion, these men confirm for themselves--rather than proving to others--that they possess some of the most important human virtues. Thus they make evident the extraordinary strength of their sense of self and their ease with their own selves. In each of these qualities one recognizes a different aspect of the fixed conception of self-worth that inheres in these men. Quiet satisfaction, pride, inner strength, and a genuine expressiveness without effusiveness here coalesce in a type of masculinity that is certainly more widespread in reality then in sociology. Slim and his sitting buddies have created a caring community that crosses boundaries of race. The men transcend the usual limits of the male role. They are vulnerable and expressive while living with resolve and remaining directed by standards within themselves.■

NOTES

NOTES

CHAPTER 7

Deviance, Crime, and Social Control

Objectives

In this chapter, you will learn about the social nature of deviance and the way society attempts to limit deviance and promote conformity. You will study different theories of crime, comparing the biological, psychological, and sociological explanations of criminal behavior.

Here are some of the questions you may want to raise:

1. What is the social origin of deviance?

2. Why do people commit crimes? Why are some people hardened criminals?

3. Can society effectively exercise social control? Is there a best way to do that?

4. Will the certainty of punishment prevent most people from committing crimes? Does jail serve any purpose? Are there alternatives?

5. What are the different types of crime? Are they equally likely to be punished?

6. How do the sociological perspectives explain the increased level of crime in our society?

7. Are some groups in our society more likely to commit crimes and/or be the victims of crime?

8. How well is our criminal justice system working?

Your own questions:

UNDERSTANDING YOUR OWN TEXTBOOK READING

1. Write a list of behaviors that would fit your definition of:

   crime:

   deviance:

   conformity:

2. What was the basis for your categories?

3. What do deviance and crime have in common? Are all deviant behaviors criminal behaviors?

4. Define Durkheim's concept of <u>anomie</u>. How is it related to criminal behavior?

5. What is another name for Merton's theory of deviance?

6. Name two deviant behaviors that would fit each category in Merton's typology.

7. What criticisms may be validly made of Merton's theory of deviance?

8. Name the different types of crime and give an example of each.

9. Early thinkers blamed deviance on _____.

10. Take a close look at the crime statistics given in your textbook. What do they say about crime in our society?

11. Give a brief profile of people most likely to be convicted for index crimes. How do you explain such a profile?

12. According to the functionalist perspective, what are the functions and dysfunctions of deviance?

13. What types of crime does the conflict perspective best explain?

14. What do the labeling and conflict perspectives have in common?

TESTING YOUR KNOWLEDGE

True and False

1. All crimes are deviant acts.   T F

2. Social control is always directly applied to prevent crime.   T F

3. Vagrancy laws were enacted to serve the interests of the poor.   T F

4. In general, people are more likely to be victimized by violent crimes than by property crimes.   T F

5. Among industrialized countries, the U.S. has the highest rate of violent crimes.   T F

6. White females and elderly people are the most often victimized in our society.   T F

7. Human beings fit into distinct criminal versus non-criminal categories.   T F

8. The people described in arrest, jail, and prison statistics tend to be predominantly male and disproportionately young and black.   T F

9. According to Merton, conformity is a common response among people in anomic situations.   T F

10. According to the labeling perspective on deviance, messages given to deviant people, including punishment, enhance rather than decrease deviant behavior.   T F

Multiple Choice

1. Informal sanctions can be applied through: _____
   a. gesture, frowns, praises, gossips
   b. companionship
   c. violence
   d. all of the above

2. Receiving a diploma or winning a gold medal are examples of: _____
   a. formal positive sanction
   b. informal positive sanction
   c. both a. and b.
   d. none of the above

3. In victimless crimes, the only victims are: _____
   a. the state
   b. the offender
   c. any witness to the crime
   d. none of the above

4. According to Merton, people who accept the norms of society but reject its socially prescribed means are: _____
   a. innovators
   b. retreatists
   c. ritualists
   d. rebellious

5. According to Emile Durkheim, anomie can be seen as a result of: _____
   a. people's laziness
   b. differential association
   c. rapid social changes
   d. an increase in poverty

6. The term "white-collar crime" was coined by: _____
   a. Robert Merton
   b. Emile Durkheim
   c. the FBI
   d. Edwin Sutherland

7. The labeling perspective on deviance is related to: _____
   a. the interactionist and conflict perspectives
   b. the functionalist and conflict perspectives
   c. the functionalist and interactionist perspectives
   d. corporate crime and organized crime

8. The relative absence of legal restrictions against socially destructive elite behavior is a contention of: _____
    a. the conflict perspective
    b. the interactionist perspective
    c. the functionalist perspective
    d. the labeling perspective

9. Deviance reflects the failure to understand the common social interests that bind all members of society is a contention of: _____
    a. the conflict perspective
    b. the labeling perspective
    c. the functionalist perspective
    d. the interactionist perspective

10. Bias in the U.S. justice system leads to differential sentencing for: _____
    a. white criminals only
    b. Black and Hispanic criminals
    c. all racial groups equally
    d. only the most hardened criminals, regardless of their ethnic origin

ESSAY PRACTICE

1. Write a brief explanation and critique of the <u>structural contradiction</u> theory of deviance.

2. Explain the labeling perspective on crime. What categories does it best explain?

CRITICAL THINKING EXERCISES

1. Briefly describe the various types of crime and give two current or recent examples of each.

2. Why is the rate of violent crime so high in the U.S.? What could be done to reduce the level of criminal behavior?

DIFFERENTIAL ASSOCIATION
Edwin H. Sutherland

The scientific explanation of a phenomenon may be stated either in terms of the factors which are operating at the moment of the occurrence of a phenomenon or in terms of the processes operating in the earlier history of that phenomenon. In the first case the explanation is mechanistic, in the second historical or genetic; both are usable. The physical and biological scientists favor the first of these methods, and it would probably be superior as an explanation of criminal behavior. Efforts at explanations of the mechanistic type have been notably unsuccessful, perhaps largely because they have been concentrated on the attempt to isolate personal and social pathologies. Work from this point of view has, at least, resulted in the conclusion that the immediate factors in criminal behavior lie in the person-situation complex. Person and situation are not factors exclusive of each other, for the situation which is important is the situation as defined by the person who is involved. The tendencies and inhibitions at the moment of the criminal behavior are, to be sure, largely a product of the earlier history of the person, but the expression of these tendencies and inhibitions is a reaction to the immediate situation as defined by the person. The situation operated in many ways, of which perhaps the least important is the provision of an opportunity for a criminal act. A thief may steal from perhaps the least important is the provision of an opportunity for a criminal act. A thief may steal from a fruit stand when the owner is not in sight but refrain when the owner is in sight; a bank burglar may attack a bank which is poorly protected by watchmen and burglar alarms. A corporation which manufactures automobiles seldom or never violates the Pure Food and Drug Law, but a meat-packing corporation violates this law with great frequency.

The second type of criminal behavior is made in terms of the life experience of a person and is a historical or genetic explanation of criminal behavior. This, to be sure, assumes a situation to be defined by the person in terms of the inclinations and abilities which the person has acquired up to that date. The following paragraphs state such a genetic theory [i.e., the theory of differential association] of criminal behavior on the assumption that a criminal act occurs when a situation appropriate for it, as defined by a person, is present.

(1) *Criminal behavior is learned.* Negatively, this means that criminal behavior is not inherited, as such; also, the person who is not already trained in crime does not invent criminal behavior, just as a person does not make mechanical inventions unless he has had training in mechanics.

(2) *Criminal behavior is learned in interaction with other persons in a process of communication.* This communication is verbal in many respects but includes also "the communication of gestures."

(3) *The principal part of the learning of criminal behavior occurs within intimate personal groups.* Negatively, this means that the impersonal agencies of communication, such as picture shows and newspapers, play a relatively unimportant part in the genesis of criminal behavior.

(4) *When criminal behavior is learned, the learning includes* (a) *techniques of committing the crime, which are sometimes very complicated, sometimes very simple;* (b) *the specific direction of motives, drives, rationalizations, and attitudes.*

(5) *The specific direction of motives and drives is learned from definitions of legal codes as favorable and unfavorable.* In some societies an individual is surrounded by persons who invariably define the legal codes as rules to be observed, whereas in others he is surrounded by persons whose definitions are favorable to the violation of the legal codes. In our American society these definitions are almost always mixed, and consequently we have culture conflict in relation to the legal codes.

(6) *A person becomes delinquent because of an excess of definitions favorable to violation of law over definitions unfavorable to violation of law.* This is the principle of differential association. It refers to both criminal and anti-criminal associations and has to do with counteracting forces. When persons become criminals, they do so because of contacts with criminal patterns and also because of isolation from anti-criminal patterns. Any persons inevitably assimilates the surrounding culture unless other patterns are in conflict; a Southerner does not pronounce "r" because Southerners do not pronounce "r." Negatively, this proposition of differential association means that associations which are neutral so far as crime is concerned have little or no effect on the genesis of criminal behavior. Much of the experience of a person is neutral in this sense, e.g., learning to brush one's teeth. This behavior is important especially as an occupier of the time of a child so that he is not in contact with criminal behavior during the time he is engaged in neutral behavior.

(7) *Differential associations may vary in frequency, duration, priority, and intensity.* This means that associations with criminal behavior and also associations with anti-criminal behavior vary in those respects. "Frequency" and "duration" as modalities of associations are obvious and need no explanation. "Priority" is assumed to be important in the sense that lawful behavior developed in early childhood may persist throughout life, and also that delinquent behavior developed in early childhood may persist throughout life. This tendency, however, has not been adequately demonstrated, and priority seems to be important principally through its selective influence. "Intensity" is not precisely defined, but it has to do with such things as the prestige of the source of a criminal or anti-criminal pattern and with emotional reactions related to the associations. In a precise description of the criminal behavior of a person these modalities would be stated in quantitative form and a mathematical ratio be reached. A formula in this sense has not been developed, and the development of such a formula would be extremely difficult.

(8) *The process of learning criminal behavior by association with criminal and anti-criminal patterns involves all of the mechanisms that are involved in any other learning.* Negatively, this means that the learning of criminal behavior is not restricted to the process of imitation. A person who is seduced, for instance, learns criminal behavior by association, but the process would not ordinarily be described as imitation.

(9) *Though criminal behavior is an expression of general needs and values, it is not explained by those general needs and values since non-criminal behavior is an expression of the same needs and values.* Thieves generally steal in order to secure money, but likewise honest laborers work in order to secure money. The attempts by many scholars to explain criminal behavior by general drives and values, such as the happiness principle, striving for social status, the money motive, or frustration, have been and must continue to be futile since they explain lawful behavior as completely as they explain criminal behavior. They are similar to respiration, which is necessary for any behavior but which does not differentiate criminal from non-criminal behavior.

It is not necessary, on this level of discussion, to explain why a person has the associations which he has; this certainly involves a complex of many things. In an area where the delinquency rate is high a boy who is sociable, gregarious, active, and athletic is very likely to come in contact with the other boys in the neighborhood, learn delinquent behavior from them, and become a gangster; in the same neighborhood the psychopathic boy who is isolated, introvert, and inert may remain at home, not become acquainted with the other boys in the neighborhood, and not become delinquent. In another situation, the sociable, athletic, aggressive boy may become a member of a scout troop and not become involved in delinquent behavior. The person's associations are determined in a general context of social organization. A child is ordinarily reared in a family; the place of residence of the family ids determined largely by family income; and the delinquency rate is in many respects related to the rental value of the houses. Many other factors enter into this social organization, including many personal group relationships.

The preceding explanation of criminal behavior was stated from the point of view of the person who engages in criminal behavior. It is also possible to state theories of criminal behavior from the point of view of the community, nation, or other group. The problem, when thus stated, is generally concerned with crime rates and involves a comparison of the crime rates of various groups or the crime rates of a particular group at different times. One of the best explanations of crime rates from this point of view is that a high crime rate is due to social disorganization. The term "social disorganization" is not entirely satisfactory, and it seems preferable to substitute for it the term "differential social organization." The postulate on which this theory is based, regardless of the name, is that crime is rooted in the social organization and is an expression of that social organization. A group may be organized for criminal behavior or organized against criminal behavior. Most communities are organized both for criminal and anti-criminal behavior, and in that sense the crime rate is an expression of the differential group organization. Differential group organization as an explanation of a crime rate must be consistent with the explanation of the criminal behavior of the person, since the crime rate is a summary statement of the number of persons in the group who commit crimes and the frequency with which they commit crimes.■

NOTES

CHAPTER 8

Social Stratification

Objectives

This chapter analyzes the division of people in socio-economic class, with the resultant inequality of duties and privileges. It focuses on the economic, status, and power dimensions, social mobility, and poverty in America. The functionalist and conflict perspectives offer a useful framework for understanding these issues.

Here are some questions you may want to raise:

1. Is social inequality found in all societies?

2. How do we explain the unequal distribution of wealth, status, and power in our society?

3. Why are some groups of people persistently poor and powerless?

4. Is poverty an individual or a social problem? Can it be eliminated? If so, how?

5. How do the sociological perspectives attempt to explain inequality? Is any of them more convincing?

6. What is power? Who has it and how is it exercised to allocate privileges in our society?

7. Can social inequality be eliminated?

8. With regard to socio-economic inequality, how do we compare with other advanced countries?

Your own questions:

UNDERSTANDING YOUR OWN TEXTBOOK READING

1. Social stratification is also called:

   It can be defined as:

2. What is the difference between <u>income</u> and <u>wealth</u>?

3. Briefly define and give examples of each:

   an open stratification system:

   a caste system:

   an estate system:

   a class system:

4. List Max Weber's three dimensions of stratification:

   1.
   2.
   3.

5. In Karl Marx's analysis of capitalism, the bourgeoisie is _____,

   whereas the proletariat is _____.

6. Give an example each of:

   intergenerational mobility:

   horizontal mobility:

   vertical mobility:

7. List the consequences of stratification in the United States.

8. The category of long term poor people is called _____.

9. List the groups with disproportionate degrees of poverty in the U.S.

10. The single biggest risk factor for poverty is _____.

11. When the causes of poverty are attributed to the people themselves, what characteristics are usually given to them?

12. Describe how the "poverty level" is established in the United States.

TESTING YOUR KNOWLEDGE

True and False

1. Some form of social stratification is found in all societies.   T F

2. Social class is a key determinant of people's values.   T F

3. Max Weber took a one-dimensional approach to social stratification.   T F

4. The United States has less income inequality than most other developed countries.   T F

5. Conflict theorists view competition for scarce resources as the basis for social inequality.   T F

6. In stratification terminology, <u>esteem</u> refers to the occupation, while <u>prestige</u> refers to the individual.   T F

7. The term social mobility refers to movements of individuals to a higher position.   T F

8. The majority of poor people are poor because they are too lazy to work.   T F

9. Ascribed statuses, such as race and gender are not important in class societies.   T F

10. Social class has nothing to do with life chances.   T F

Multiple Choice

1. Income differences in the United States are: _____
   a. very large
   b. a bit large
   c. insignificant
   d. irrelevant to people's life chances

2. A caste system is: _____
   a. an open stratification system
   b. a closed stratification system
   c. an upward mobility system
   d. a downward mobility system

3. The highest degree of social mobility is found in the: _____
   a. caste system
   b. class system
   c. estate system
   d. none of the above

4. Class systems are predominantly based on: _____
   a. ascribed statuses
   b. achieved statuses
   c. master statuses
   d. no status at all

5. The social thinker who made the most important early contribution to the concept of social class is: _____
   a. Max Weber
   b. Charles Murray
   c. Emile Durkheim
   d. Karl Marx

6. In sociology, power can be defined as: _____
   a. the ability to affect the actions of others
   b. the ability to impose one's will against the will of others
   c. the ability to make decisions that affect the direction of the entire society
   d. all of the above

7. Class consciousness and false consciousness were concepts originally defined by: _____
   a. Max Weber
   b. Karl Marx
   c. Daniel Rossides
   d. none of the above

8. Vertical mobility relates to: _____
    a. intergenerational mobility
    b. intragenerational mobility
    c. all of the above
    d. none of the above

9. _____ is an important factor in intergenerational mobility in American society today.
    a. luck
    b. education
    c. a powerful acquaintance
    d. a stable family life

10. The fact that women are more likely than men to fall below the poverty level results in what sociologists call: _____
    a. women's economic decadence
    b. women's ascribed status
    c. the feminization of poverty
    d. the Murray Thesis on poverty

ESSAY PRACTICE

1. Describe and analyze the American system of social stratification. Use the statistical information from your textbook.

2. Compare the functionalist and conflict perspectives on social stratification.

CRITICAL THINKING EXERCISES

1. After debating the respective arguments of the functionalist and conflict perspectives, decide which one provides a better understanding of the American class system.

2. Discuss the restrictions to social mobility in our present society.

3. Do you share the view that "the United States is slowly moving toward a bipolar income distribution"?

4. How can you explain the rise of homelessness in our affluent society? How can homelessness be eliminated?

SOME PRINCIPLES OF STRATIFICATION
Kingsley Davis and Wilbert E. Moore

In a previous paper some concepts for handling the phenomena of social inequality were presented. In the present paper a further step in stratification theory is undertaken--an attempt to show the relationship between stratification and the rest of the social order. Starting from the proposition that no society is "classless," or unstratified, and effort is made to explain, in functional terms, the universal necessity which calls forth stratification in any social system. Next, an attempt is made to explain the roughly uniform distribution of prestige as between the major types of positions in every society. Since, however, there occur between one society and another great differences in the degree and kind of stratification, some attention is also given to the varieties of social inequality and the variable factors that give rise to them.

Clearly, the present task requires two different lines of analysis--one to understand the universal, the other to understand the variable features of stratification. Naturally each line of inquiry aids the other and is indispensable, and in the treatment that follows the two will be interwoven, although, because of space limitations, the emphasis will be on the universals.

Throughout, it will be necessary to keep in mind one thing--namely, that the discussion relates to the system of positions, not to the individuals occupying those positions. It is one thing to ask why different positions carry different degrees of prestige, and quite another to ask how certain individuals get into those positions. Although, as the argument will try to show, both questions are related, it is essential to keep them separate in our thinking. Most of the literature on stratification has tried to answer the second question (particularly of mobility between strata) without tackling the first. The first question, however, is logically prior and, in the case of any particular individual or group, factually prior.

THE FUNCTIONAL NECESSITY OF STRATIFICATION

Curiously, however, the main functional necessity explaining the universal presence of stratification is precisely the requirement faced by any society of placing and motivating individuals in the social structure. As a functioning mechanism a society must somehow distribute its members with motivation at two different levels: to instill in the proper individuals the desire to fill certain positions, and, once in these positions, the desire to perform the duties attached to them. Even though the social order may be relatively static in form, there is a continuous process of metabolism as new individuals are born into it, shift with age, and die off. The absorption into the positional system must somehow be arranged and motivated. This is true whether the system is competitive or non-competitive. A competitive system gives greater importance to the motivation to achieve positions, whereas a non-competitive system gives perhaps greater importance to the motivation to perform the duties of the positions; but in any system both types of motivation are required.

If the duties associated with the various positions were all equally pleasant to the human organism, all equally important to societal survival, and all equally in need of the same ability or talent, it would make no difference who got into which positions, and the problem of social placement would be greatly reduced. But actually it does make a great deal of difference who gets into which position, not only because some positions are inherently more agreeable than others, but also because some require special talents or training and some are functionally more important than others. Also, it is essential that the duties of the positions be performed with the diligence that their importance requires. Inevitably, then, a society must have, first, some kinds of rewards that it can use as inducements, and second, some way of distributing these rewards differentially according to positions. The rewards and their distributions become a part of the social order and thus give rise to stratification.

One may ask what kind of rewards a society has at its disposal in distributing its personnel and securing essential services. It has, first of all, the things that contribute to sustenance and comfort. It has, second, the things that contribute to humor and diversion. And it has, finally, the things that contribute to self respect and ego expansion. The last, because of the peculiarly social character of the self, is largely a function of the opinion of others, but it nonetheless ranks in importance with the first two. In any social system all three kinds of rewards must be dispersed differentially according to positions.

In a sense the rewards are "built into" the position. They consist in the "rights" associated with the position, plus what may be called its accompaniments or perquisites. Often the rights, and sometimes the accompaniments, are functionally related to the duties of the position (rights as viewed by the incumbent are usually duties as viewed by other members of the community). However, there may be a host of subsidiary rights and perquisites that are not essential to the function of the position and have only an indirect and symbolic connection with its duties, but which still may be of considerable importance in inducing people to seek the positions and fulfill the essential duties.

If the rights and perquisites of different positions in a society must be unequal, then the society must be stratified, because that is precisely what stratification means. Social inequality is thus an unconsciously evolved device by which societies insure that the most important positions are conscientiously filled by the most qualified persons. Hence every society, no matter how simple or complex, must differentiate persons in terms of both prestige and esteem, and must therefore possess a certain amount of institutionalized inequality.

It does not follow that the amount or type of inequality need be the same in all societies. This is largely a function of factors that will be discussed presently.

THE TWO DETERMINANTS OF POSITIONAL RANK

Granting the general function that inequality subserves, one can specify the two factors that determine the relative rank of different positions. In general those positions convey the best reward, and hence have the highest rank, which (a) have the greatest importance for the society and (b) require the greatest training or talent. The first factor concerns function and is a matter of relative significance; the second concerns means and is a matter of scarcity.

Differential Functional Importance Actually a society does not need to reward positions in proportion to their functional importance. It merely needs to give sufficient reward to them to insure that they will be filled competently. In other words, it must see that less essential positions do not compete successfully with more essential ones. If a position is easily filled, it need not be heavily rewarded, even though important. On the other hand, if it is important but hard to fill, the reward must be high enough to get it filled anyway. Functional importance is therefore a necessary but not a sufficient cause of high rank being assigned to a position.

Differential Scarcity of Personnel Practically all positions, no matter how acquired, require some form of skill or capacity for performance. This is implicit in the very notion of position, which implies that the incumbent must, by virtue of his incumbency, accomplish certain things.

There are, ultimately, only two ways in which a person's qualifications come about: through inherent capacity or through training. Obviously, in concrete activities both are always necessary, but from a practical standpoint the scarcity may lie primarily in one or the other, as well as in both. Some positions require innate talents of such high degree that the persons who fill them are bound to be rare. In many cases, however, talent is fairly abundant in the population but the training example, is within the mental capacity of most individuals, but a medical education is so burdensome and expensive that virtually none would undertake it if the position of the M.D. did not carry a reward commensurate with the sacrifice.

If the talents required for a position are abundant and the training easy, the method of acquiring the position may have little to do with its duties. There may be, in fact, a virtually accidental relationship. But if the skills required are scarce by reason of the rarity of talent or the costliness of training, the position, if functionally important, must have an attractive power that will draw the necessary skills in competition with other positions. This means, in effect, that the position must be high in the social scale--must command great prestige, high salary, ample leisure, and the like.■

NOTES

CHAPTER 9

World Stratification

Objectives

This chapter presents a picture of world stratification, or the division of the countries of the world along various degrees of economic wealth, political power, and technological achievements. It explores some theories which attempt to explain the nature of the relationship between developed and developing nations, and the impact of the world political and economic systems on the widening gap between rich and poor countries.

Here are some questions you may want to raise:

1. Why are some countries so persistently poor and seemingly unable to improve their economic and social conditions?

2. Why are there famine and starvation in some parts of the world, while other countries enjoy so much luxury?

3. How do domestic and international politics impact on economic development?

4. What is the long-term consequence of global stratification?

5. How can the more advanced nations help the poorer ones?

Your own questions:

UNDERSTANDING YOUR OWN TEXTBOOK READING

1. How has the world stratification system changed over the past 25 years?

2. Explain the division of the world in "first," "second," and "third" worlds. Why does such division appear to be obsolete today?

3. How does the World Bank classify the world countries?

4. Name the <u>social causes</u> of famine and starvation in some parts of the world today.

5. How do the "market oriented" theories relate to the "modernization" theory?

6. According to the "modernization theory", how can low-income countries break out of poverty? Briefly evaluate this theory.

7. Why are Marxist theorists also called "dependency" theorists?

8. According to Brazilian sociologist Fernando Cardozo, how is <u>dependent development</u> possible?

9. Explain Wallerstein's three-level division of the world economic system.

10. Explain the causes of economic growth in the newly industrializing countries (NICs).

TESTING YOUR KNOWLEDGE

True and False

1. In poor countries, men and women suffer equally. T F

2. Climate changes have resulted in widespread famine in Africa. T F

3. Food production in the world as a whole continues to decrease. T F

4. The effects of natural disasters (hurricanes, floods, etc.) vary with the social conditions of the potential victims. T F

5. Colonialism was established to improve the conditions of the colonized people. T F

6. Governments have no significant role to play in the economic development of the developing countries. T F

7. The Confucian cultural heritage stresses the value of hard work. T F

8. In many ways, Taiwan, Korea, Hong Kong, and Singapore benefited from their colonial relationships with Japan and Great Britain. T F

9. The theory of the New International Division of Labor is an offshoot of the World Systems theory. T F

10. The notion of commodity chain refers to agricultural activities in less developed countries. T F

Multiple Choice

1. The average person in a typical high-income nation has _____ times the income of his/her counterpart in the typical low-income nation.

    a. five
    b. twenty
    c. fifty-six
    d. seventy-five

2. The argument that low-income nations are not underdeveloped but misdeveloped as a result of exploitation by the wealthier nations is a contention of: _____

    a. Marxist theorists
    b. functionalist theorists
    c. market-oriented theorists
    d. interactionist theorists

3. One way to determine the wealth of a country is to measure: _____

    a. the size of its land
    b. the size of its army
    c. the size of its population
    d. its per-person gross national product

4. According to World System theories, core activities are those: _____

    a. where the profits are made
    b. from which the profits are taken
    c. that occur in the central part of the country
    d. that most people have to perform

5. Modernization and other market-oriented theories originated in: _____

    a. low-income countries
    b. Ghana and other African nations
    c. high-income industrial nations
    d. the newly industrializing countries

6. Dependency theorists typically advocate: _____

    a. increase in U.S. foreign aid
    b. elimination of foreign corporations in their countries
    c. more imports of goods in their countries
    d. a stronger world currency

7. During the past 25 years, the average per-person economic growth in South Korea was: _____

    a. one-fourth that of the U.S.
    b. one-half that of the U.S.
    c. at the same level as the U.S.
    d. about four times that of the U.S.

8. The relocation of factories to low-wage countries has mostly benefited: _____

    a. the West Indian countries
    b. the East Asian countries
    c. Africa
    d. South America

9. The fastest growing major economic region in the world today is in: _____

    a. the People's Republic of China
    b. South Africa
    c. the U.S.
    d. the northern part of Italy

10. The spread of capitalist economy at the global level may result in: _____

    a. a lowering of the standard of living in the advanced nations
    b. a world-wide economic growth that benefits everyone
    c. a leveling-off of income differences in the world
    d. all of the above

ESSAY PRACTICE

1. Write a brief comparison of rich and poor nations along the dimensions of: population; wealth and poverty; health; education; and energy consumption.

2. Summarize the sociological lessons to be learned from the East Asian newly industrializing countries (NICs).

CRITICAL THINKING EXERCISES

1. Debate the role of transnational corporations in world stratification.

2. Present your own scenario of global economic, social, and political conditions fifty years from now.

NOTES

NOTES

CHAPTER 10

Race and Ethnic Relations

Objectives

This chapter analyzes the sociological implications of race and ethnicity and the dynamics of race and ethnic relations. Problems of racial and ethnic conflicts are explored at the national and international levels.

Here are some of the questions you may want to raise:

1. Why are race and ethnicity given such importance in human relations?

2. Is racial inequality a universal phenomenon?

3. Is conflict a necessary consequence of racial and ethnic diversity?

4. What are alternative responses to cultural diversity?

5. What is racism and what are its causes and effects?

6. What are the sociological perspectives on race relations? How useful are they in helping us understand our society?

7. Is America moving toward more racial and ethnic conflicts or toward ultimate racial harmony?

8. If racial harmony is possible in our society, how will it be achieved?

Your own questions:

UNDERSTANDING YOUR OWN TEXTBOOK READING

1. Explain how the following are <u>social</u>, rather than <u>biological</u> or <u>numerical</u> concepts:

    race:

    ethnic group:

    majority/minority groups:

    racism:

2. Establish the difference between <u>prejudice</u> and <u>discrimination</u>. How are these concepts related?

3. Give two examples each of individual prejudice, individual discrimination, and institutional discrimination.

4. Give two examples each of <u>scapegoating</u> and <u>stereotyping</u>. How are these two processes linked to prejudice, discrimination, and racial violence?

5. List the dysfunctions associated with racism:

6. What is the difference between <u>assimilation</u> and <u>pluralism</u>?

7. Name the factors which have influenced the flow of immigrants to the U.S.

8. How is the status of the American Indians different from that of other minority groups?

9. Explain how the "Jim Crow" laws affected the conditions of African Americans.

10. Use statistical figures to explain the gains of African Americans today compared to the pre-civil rights period. Why are there still widespread dissatisfaction among this minority group?

11. What advantages did the Cuban immigrants have over other Latino groups?

12. Explain the economic success of many Asian Americans.

TESTING YOUR KNOWLEDGE

True and False

1. Every human being can be clearly placed in one of three races: Caucasoid, Negroid, and Mongoloid.   T F

2. The most subtle form of racism, yet perhaps the one with the most serious consequences today, is individual discrimination.   T F

3. Stereotypes are always negative.   T F

4. Racism is a form of prejudice.   T F

5. Institutional discrimination against Black Americans goes back to the institution of slavery in the U.S.   T F

6. <u>Amalgamation</u> is another word form <u>assimilation</u>.   T F

7. Getting rid of active discrimination if enough to crate truly equal opportunity.   T F

8. Only Africans were brought to the American colonies in servitude.   T F

9. During the colonial period of the seventeenth and eighteenth centuries, as many Africans as Europeans arrived in the American colonies.   T F

10. Between 1870 and 1901, only one African American served in the U.S. Congress.   T F

11. The American Indians form a homogeneous cultural group.   T F

12. Racial housing segregation and discrimination are found only in the United States.   T F

Multiple Choice

1. Race is based on _____, while ethnicity is based on _____ factors.

    a. cultural; biological
    b. physical; cultural
    c. biological; physical
    d. cultural; status

2. For both race ad ethnic groups, membership is: _____

    a. an achieved status
    b. an ascribed status
    c. a conscious decision
    d. a lifelong choice

3. An important function of ideological racism is: _____

    a. to create inequality in society
    b. to provoke conflict in order to bring about change
    c. to maintain equilibrium in the social system
    d. to justify or rationalize the exploitation of a minority group

4. In 1882, Congress passed a law forbidding immigration of this racial group: _____

    a. Japanese
    b. Chinese
    c. West Indian
    d. Mexican

5. The largest ethnic minority group in the United States is made of: _____

    a. the Hispanics and Latinos
    b. the African Americans
    c. the Japanese
    d. the Jews

6. Most immigrants entering the United States today are: _____

    a. Eastern Europeans
    b. Western Europeans
    c. Hispanics and Asians
    d. Russians

7. This group is stereotyped as the "model minority." _____

    a. Asian
    b. German
    c. Irish
    d. Jewish

8. Between 1820 and 1991, the largest population of immigrants to the U.S. were: _____
   a. Latin Americans
   b. Asians
   c. Europeans
   d. Philippinos

9. They have the highest rate of poverty among the Latinos: _____
   a. the Mexican Americans
   b. the Puerto Ricans
   c. the Cubans
   d. the Dominicans

10. Globalization has brought with it: _____
    a. an increase in acts of racial and ethnic violence
    b. a decrease in acts of racial and ethnic violence
    c. more racial harmony in the world
    d. none of the above

ESSAY PRACTICE

1. Why have attempts to classify human beings into a neatly established set of races never produced consistent results?

2. How is racism manifested in American society today? How can it be eliminated?

CRITICAL THINKING EXERCISES

1. Do you agree with the statement that "today, institutional discrimination is often unconscious and unintentional, though its consequences can be just as devastating as if it were deliberate."? (Farley, 1988, 305).

2. Identify the different ways the dominant group in America has responded to the different minority groups living in the country. Do you see a relationship between these responses and the present socio-economic conditions of these groups?

RACISM: DENIAL AND PERPETUATION
Martin Lee and Norman Solomon

Public images of racial minorities are still largely controlled by whites in American mass media. Newsrooms regularly foster unbalanced reporting about people of color. The patterns may go unnoticed because they're so routine.

America has been called a nation of immigrants--but the news media, through language and emphasis, often give the impression that some immigrants are more welcome than others. For Hispanic people in the United States, much of the media focus is on law enforcement actions against undocumented workers, who are often listed as contributors to the nation's woes. Under the headline "US Paying Stiff Price for Porous Borders," the *Christian Science Monitor* printed this subhead on its front page: "After three centuries of inattention, pressure is building to close off entry of drugs, aliens." The article's first sentence grouped together "drug traffickers, illegal aliens, smugglers, and even potential terrorists."

Likely to evoke sci-fi images at least unconsciously, the phrase "illegal aliens"--standard in the news--is dehumanizing. Linda Mitchell, spokeswoman for the Coalition for Humane Immigrant Rights of Lost Angeles, calls that catch-phrase "an inflammatory way to categorize a group of people. It's a polarizing term. An alien is someone who's not human, so the message is we don't need to care about how they're being treated. The use of these words in the media ends up justifying how people are looked at: 'Illegal Aliens' don't have rights because they're criminals and it's as if they're from another planet."

Customarily obscured are some key reasons why undocumented workers have come to the U.S. from south of the border. Nearly a half-million Salvadoran refugees settled in the Los Angeles area during the 1980s; news accounts rarely connected the exodus from their war-wracked homeland with massive U.S. military aid to the government of El Salvador. Nor is the press inclined to link the influx of Mexicans to their country's debt crisis and economic tailspins--even though U.S. policies have more than a little to do with those circumstances.

While posing as foes of prejudice, the mainstream media do much to sustain it. Writing in *Essence* magazine, journalist Jeri L. Love charged that the country's mass communications system "exhibits continuous indifference, ignorance and insensitivity toward the Black community." The same goes for Native Americans, and many Latino and Asian communities. Love's judgment may seem unduly harsh to those who prefer to believe that mass media side with racial understanding and social justice. But that very impression is a dangerous result of news media that have been more self-congratulatory than candid about current racial realities in the United States.

RACISM AT THE TOP

Despite periodic flaps about racist statements by public figures, the mass media seem willing to accept racism in high places. The political career of Ronald Reagan is a case in point. During the battle for "open housing" in California, when blacks sought the right to live in neighborhoods of their choice, then-Governor Reagan maintained that the blacks were "just making trouble" and really had no intention of moving. When Martin Luther King, Jr. was killed in 1968, Reagan implied that King had brought the assassination upon himself that by breaking unjust laws in the interest of desegregation, King had somehow given the green light to murder. When poor blacks gathered in Oakland to receive free groceries paid as ransom in the 1974 kidnapping of Patty Hearst, Reagan quipped that he hoped for "and outbreak of botulism" among the food recipients. Media did not make an issue of these statements when Reagan ran for the presidency. Moreover, in 1982, President Reagan wrote a letter praising the publisher of overtly racist and anti-Semitic literature, Roger Pearson, but that was no big deal as far as news media were concerned.

During the 1984 and 1988 campaigns, however, the press kept after Jesse Jackson to atone for his "Hymietown" remark (which he did on numerous occasions) and to repudiate black nationalist minister Louis Farrakhan for making anti-Semitic remarks. But the media still did not hold Reagan and George Bush accountable for their tolerance of racism, even though a Reagan Cabinet member, Terrell Bell, said that racist slurs were frequently uttered by White House staffers. When Interior Secretary James Watt's racist remarks led to his resignation, the White House expressed regrets over his departure--and the media let the matter drop rather than push Reagan to denounce Watt.

Nor did the mass media confront the racist remarks that House Republican leader Robert Michel uttered nearly two months before the 1988 general election. In a TV interview taped in mid-September--but kept under wraps until six days after the election, when *USA Today: The Television Show* finally broadcast it--Michel stated that he wished he could use the word "nigger" in the song "Ol' Man River." Michel also expressed regret at the dying out of minstrel shows, and rendered an impromptu imitation of Kingfish from *Amos 'n' Andy*. Yet USA Today's TV show did not consider his statements to be "news" until after the election was over. Even when the interview was aired, most national media treated it as a minor story that ended with Michel's perfunctory apology. "If a right-winger says something really insulting, it's treated as just another day at the race track," an aide to a black member of Congress told the Guardian. "But if a black says something insensitive, it's considered a matter of stirring up racial animosities."

Michel went on making widely-quoted statements and writing prominent articles about congressional "ethics"--his stature and ability to do so undiminished. To many in the mass media, questions of racism do not qualify as matters of "ethics."

During George Bush's successful campaign for the White House, mass media saw to it that most voters never found out about his Caucasian-only housing covenants in Texas. On February 4, 1981, after he became Vice President, Bush bought a lot in West Oaks, Texas, as the site of a future retirement home in the all-white neighborhood. Bush signed a contract with a clause that the land could not "be sold, leased, or rented to any person other than of the Caucasian race, except in the case of servant's quarters." In late 1987 *The Nation* exposed the story of Bush's racially restrictive deed--and several others he had signed since the 1950s. The magazine reported that a spokesperson for Bush said, "There's really nothing to this." Mass media agreed. It stayed a non-issue.

MINORITIES IN NEWSROOMS

Inside journalism, on a systematic basis, white people retain a disproportionate share of the power. That imbalance affects how the news gets reported every day. "Even when stories dealt with bald-faced injustices and black-community disenchantment," Kirk Johnson concluded in his study of Boston's mass media, "most reporters refused to acknowledge racism as an underlying mechanism. Indeed, the very word 'racism' was rarely uttered in the major media; when racism was mentioned, it was treated not as a continuing tradition, but as a mere historical footnote. Euphemisms such as 'the disadvantaged' and 'the underprivileged' suggested a reluctance to acknowledge the persons or institutions responsible for causing the 'disadvantage.'" Victims without victimizers--a common theme in media coverage of domestic issues.

Columnist Clarence Page, who won a Pulitzer Prize for commentary in 1989, has seen a big improvement in hiring practices since he joined the Chicago Tribune news staff 20 years earlier as only its second full-time minority reporter. Yet ever at the end of the 1980s, the Tribune's daily news operation lacked black people in supervisory positions. "I think it hurts the paper as far as having sensitivity during the day to what issues are important in the black community and also what issues are developing in the black community and the Hispanic community too," he said.

One of the few Asian-Americans working as an editor on a sizable daily paper in the United States, William Wong settled into writing a regular column for the *Oakland Tribune* in 1988. Says Wong, "A lot of the things I bring up are not even talked about by other columnists."

"Chicago's news," Mayor Harold Washington contended, "never quite came out the way things actually happened. It came out in a skewed fashion because we didn't have Hispanics, women, blacks, and other minorities to winnow out, interpret, and help make the news more meaningful to the majority of people in our city." Shortly before his death, he predicted that news coverage "shall forever be biased in Chicago, until people get fed up and start demanding that something be done about it. We need to reevaluate the whole structure of the news industry--the owners, editors, anchorpersons, producers, journalists on the street."

Washington went on to say that while many policies were especially hurting black and Hispanic people, "it's difficult to get our message across when it's siphoned through newspapers and other media which in many cases are predisposed against shat we're trying to say." Speaking in 1986, Washington pointed out that in many U.S. cities the "minority" is actually a majority of the population. "Yet most metropolitan newspapers do not cater to the working public within their cities; they reach out to the suburbs to embrace a more affluent readership. These papers are still based in our cities, they own city property and to a great extent they control our cities. But newspapers largely ignore the people right around them."

Many journalists have expressed similar concerns. But the profession as a whole has moved slowly in response. The 1989 figures were hardly encouraging. "Blacks, Hispanics, Asians, and Native Americans now constitute 7.54% of all newsroom professionals, up from 7.02% last year," the American Society of Newspaper Editors announced. What's more, a majority of U.S. daily newspapers--54%--did not have a single minority person in the newsroom. And while nearly 20% of recently-hired newspaper journalists were from racial minorities, the hierarchy remained almost entirely white--95.5%.

Several months after the release of the 1989 survey results, a *New York Times* article noted that recent Supreme Court decision weakening affirmative action laws "have raised fears that expanding minority employment within news organizations may become more difficult than ever." Yet the *Times* headline gave the opposite impression: "'Sense of Muscle' for Black Journalists." The implication was that newspaper owners could hardly be expected to hire more black journalists voluntarily.

The *New York Times* managed to be somewhat sanguine, in spite of--or perhaps because of--its notably shabby record as an equal opportunity employer. A profile of the *Times*, published in the *Columbia Journalism Review* at the end of 1988, said that "despite more than 20 years of pledging to vary the color of the newsroom and despite settlement of a rancorous lawsuit eight years ago that set specific hiring and promotion goals, the paper has only six blacks who have reached positions as assistant or deputy editors or editors of special sections."

Active discrimination has been widespread--from tiny newspapers to the country's most renowned. In spring 1987, a jury found the *New York Daily News* guilty of discriminating against four black journalists on the staff. At the *Washington Post*, after 20 years of union efforts to halt discriminatory practices at the newspaper, employees filed a class-action complaint with the District of Columbia government, charging widespread bias by the Post's management.

Electronic media have been a bit better. Figures for 1988 indicated that minorities comprised 8% of the nation's news employees at commercial radio stations and 16% at commercial TV stations. But minorities held only 5% of supervisory positions in radio and 11% in TV. "The word is 'racism,'" says Linda Ellerbee. "It exists in the networks and in the media pretty much throughout."

As Barbara Reynolds of *USA Today* has observed, the fact that so many women on networks are blond and blue-eyed is a standard that "discriminates against black and Hispanic women." After two decades as a journalist, Reynolds was among the highest-ranking black women in the newspaper business in 1989, serving on the *USA Today* editorial board, editing its Inquiry page, and writing a column for the paper. "I think black women are an invisible presence," she said in an interview. "When people talk about blacks, they mean men." She pointed out that the American Society of Newspaper Editors was not even compiling employment data on women of color in the industry.

Reynolds--who has written that "minority women are laboring at the bottom rung of...newspaper ghettos"--said that despite her professional record, until recently she found herself often treaded as a non-person at work. "Just because you're in, it doesn't mean that it reverses the disparities available. Black women journalists have been ridiculed, humiliated, never a part of the old boy network. When you look at the top, many have decided to leave journalism because of the way they have been treated, in the Victorian way men treat women. We're always an afterthought." In newsrooms "the pressure is so great because of both of the hang-ups people have in our society with sexism and racism. It's a double-edged blade."

BLAMING THE VICTIMS: BLACK FAMILIES

For many children of all races, poverty is not a word but a gnawing reality. "Indeed," says Temple University professor Noel Cazenave, "there are millions of neglected and hungry children trapped in America's wretched house of mirrors, and their plight--and its real causes--have yet to become a *cause celebre* to America's white corporate media." Almost half of all black children in the United States--45%--were living in families officially below the poverty line, a 1989 study found. Congressman George Miller, chair of the committee that issued the report, said that "for America's youngest children and their families, the 1980s have been a disaster."

Miller blamed severe cuts in government help. But all the Republicans on the committee disagreed, blaming erosion of family structures and values--an explanation buttressed by decades of mass media boosterism for the idea that black families are largely responsible for problems faced by black people in America. Morton Kondracke of the *New Republic* typified the media spin when he wrote, "it is universally accepted that black poverty is heavily the result of family breakdown." Such an assertion was akin to saying that the absence of food is heavily the result of malnutrition.

In 1986, in the midst of a decade of sharply accelerated inner-city poverty, CBS broadcast a two-hour documentary by Bill Moyers, "The Vanishing Black Family: Crisis in Black America," that was widely praised by mass media. *Newsweek* proclaimed that "Bill Moyers and CBS News looked unflinchingly into the void: it's no longer only racism or an unsympathetic government that is destroying black America. The problem now lies in the black community itself, and in its failure to pass on moral values to the next generation."

The CBS documentary could be seen as an honest attempt to show the horrendous conditions of life in black ghettos. But it was expert tunnel vision, fixated on effects--unwed mothers, young black males with few job prospects, dilapidated housing--while virtually ignoring causes. As writer Barbara Omolade noted: "The concept of a pathological underclass has become the rationale for continued racism and economic injustice; in attempting to separate racial from economic inequality and [in] blaming family pathology for black people's condition, current ideology obscures the system's inability to provide jobs, decent wages, and adequate public services for the black poor."

Media stereotyping has persisted. "The incessant emphasis on the dysfunctioning of black people," says the longtime president of the National Council of Negro Women, Dorothy Height, "is simply one more attempt to show that African-Americans do not really fit into the society--that we are 'overdependent' and predominantly welfare-oriented. Quite overlooked in this equation is the fact that most black Americans are, on the contrary, overwhelmingly among the working poor."

The black family scapegoat has been invoked by politicians and news media time and again to declare limits on public responsibility for improving the oppressive circumstances that afflict millions of Americans. In the words of scientist Stephen Jay Gould: "How convenient to blame the poor and the hungry for their own condition--lest we be forced to blame our economic system or our government for an abject failure to secure a decent life for all people."

There has been some breakthrough coverage going beyond the usual blame-the-victim approach. A prime example was National Public Radio's half-hour report titled "Black Men: An Endangered Species." Produced by Phyllis Crockett, the program revealed stark truths about black America:

> "There are almost as many young black men in prison as in college."
>
> "For the first time in American history the life expectancy for black people is declining."
>
> "Murder and suicide are the two leading causes of death. A young black man...stands a one in 21 chance of being murdered before he's 44; for a white man, it's one in 133."
>
> "The suicide rate for young black men is up and rising...White men who commit suicide tend to do it when they see themselves as 'powerless' in their 50s; for black men, 'powerless in their 20s.'"
>
> "Even though black men make up only 6% of the U.S. population, half of all the men behind bars are black."
>
> "There is no federal response to what's happening to [black men] shown by the alarming rise in statistics. There are, of course, some job training programs, some education programs, but there is no focused effort on this problem."

Why are these facts so rarely articulated in major media?

THE MARTIN LUTHER KING, JR. WE DON'T SEE ON TELEVISION

The mass media tell us over and over that Martin Luther King, Jr. was the nation's most gifted civil rights leader. But they don't remind us that King, besides crusading for racial justice and harmony, was one of the toughest critics of America's economic system and foreign policy. To King, issues of race, poverty, and peace could not be separated.

Consider the film clips of King shown on TV every January when we celebrate his birthday as a national holiday. The TV footage presents a sanitized King with only one concern: desegregation. But in other speeches, late in his life, King went further, urging that people directly confront the connections between racism, poverty, and militarism. Those speeches were also filmed and recorded--but we don't see them on television or hear them on the radio or find them quoted in daily newspapers.

King explicitly linked racism and poverty at home with intervention and warfare abroad. The nation's press, which didn't like that kind of approach then any more than it does now, angrily criticized him for making such connections. For example, when King spoke out against the Vietnam War, editorials around the country faulted him for moving beyond civil rights into peace issues. In 1967, the *Detroit News* complained that "he risks his credentials as in influential civil rights leader on the questionable merits of his foreign policy statements." *Life*--then one of the nation's biggest publications--explained that King "goes beyond his personal right to dissent when he connects progress and civil rights here with a proposal that amounts to abject surrender in Vietnam." *The Washington Post* stated that King's criticism of the war "diminished his usefulness to his cause, to his country, and to his people." *Time* accused King of "demagogic slander that sounded like a script for Radio Hanoi."

King's response: "For about 12 years now, ever since the Montgomery bus boycott, I have been struggling and fighting against segregation, and I have been working too long and too hard now against segregated public accommodations to end up segregating my moral concerns, for since justice is indivisible, injustice anywhere is an affront to justice everywhere."

What's more, King pointed out, the conduct of the American government and corporations abroad could not be separated from what was going on inside our national borders. It had become all too clear that "when a nation becomes obsessed with the guns of war, social programs must inevitably suffer. We can talk about guns and butter all we want to, but when the guns are there with all of its emphasis you don't even get goo oleo. These are facts of life."

Corporate-controlled news outlets repeatedly show King's beautiful but general "I have a dream" oration, to the virtual exclusion of his later speeches--like the address in which he declared: "A true revolution of values will soon look uneasily on the glaring contrast of poverty and wealth. With righteous indignation, it will look across the seas and see individual capitalists of the West investing huge sums of money in Asia, Africa, and South America, only to take the profits out with no concern for the social betterment of the countries, and say: 'This is not just.' It will look at our alliance with the landed gentry of Latin America and say: 'This is not just.' The Western arrogance of feeling that it has everything to teach others and nothing to learn from them is not just."

Martin Luther King told an audience in early 1968 that "I never intend to adjust myself to the madness of militarism." He referred to a trend that we to remain with us, aided and abetted by media giants: "A nation that continues year after year to spend more money on military defense that on programs of social uplift is approaching spiritual death."

More than two decades after King was murdered, his truth is marching on. Many festering ills in our society correlate with American foreign policy guided by "the madness of militarism." And the same powerful media institutions distorting events at home are no more trustworthy when reporting on the rest of the world.■

NOTES

NOTES

CHAPTER 11

Sex, Gender, and Society

Objectives

This chapter deals with the social nature of sex differentiation and sex discrimination. It offers a comparative view of sex roles in different societies as well as a history of feminism and its present status in the U.S.

Here are some of the questions you may want to raise:

1. What is the difference between sex and gender?

2. What is the origin of sexism?

3. What is the extent of sex discrimination in other parts of the world?

4. Are career and home incompatible for women today?

5. How far has our society advanced in terms of sexual equality?

6. How can sexual inequality be eliminated in our society?

Your own questions:

UNDERSTANDING YOUR OWN TEXTBOOK READING

1. What is the difference between sex and gender?

2. What is the relationship between "gender role" and "gender identity"?

3. Define and give one example each of:

    gender-role socialization:

    hidden curriculum:

    patriarchy:

4. How does the functionalist perspective justify gender stratification?

5. Women entering the work force in the U.S. found that their experience was different from that of men in several ways. Explain.

6. What are the social consequences of women's employment?

7. How can institutional sexism be fought?

8. Explain the interactionist perspective on gender socialization.

9. How can it be said that minority women face a double jeopardy? Do you agree?

10. Explain the impact of influential gender-socialization agents in the American society.

11. Briefly state the original functions of gender roles. Do they still look valid today?

12. Do gender roles contribute to family cohesion? Explain.

13. How have women challenged sexism in the past two decades?

14. How can sexual inequality be reduced at home?

15. Is elimination of gender inequality foreseeable in the near future? Explain.

TESTING YOUR KNOWLEDGE

True and False

1. Biological differences play a role in the acquisition of gender identity.   T F

2. Gender identity and gender role are similar concepts.   T F

3. The media, especially television, are significant agents of gender-role socialization.   T F

4. The traditional male gender role is no longer prevalent in American society today.   T F

5. Gender stratification is found only in highly developed countries.   T F

6. There are no potential benefits to an androgynous lifestyle.   T F

7. Conflict theorists argue that gender stratification results from unequal power between men and women.   T F

8. Gender stratification hurt men as well as women.   T F

9. Married women's greater participation in the labor force has brought them greater power.   T F

10. The term "second shift" refers to women with two jobs outside the home.   T F

11. Nature, not nurture, is the prime determinant of gender-linked behavior.   T F

12. Gender based division of labor is a cultural universal.   T F

13. In general, husbands whose wives work outside the home are doing significantly more household chores and child care (on the average).   T F

14. Feminism originated in the U.S. with the women's movement of the 1960s.   T F

Multiple Choice

From Chapter 11, write down five multiple choice questions that reflect your understanding of the chapter as a whole and the important concepts included in the chapter.

ESSAY PRACTICE

1. Discuss the impact of sex-role socialization on work opportunities for women.

2. Do you see feminism as a challenge to male power?

3. Why has feminism become so influential in the industrialized world since World War II?

PROJECTS AND CRITICAL THINKING EXERCISES

1. Interview someone from another country. Find out what the gender roles are in that country, whether or not they have gone through changes, and how they compare with gender roles in the U.S.

2. What are the overt and covert manifestations of sexism in our society? Find as many as possible from news reports, newscasting, discussion with your parents, and other personal observations.

3. Conduct an informal poll among your friends, co-workers, acquaintances, etc. Find out how many:

    a. know about the content of the Equal Rights Amendment (ERA).

    b. are in favor or against it and why.

    c. do not care one way or the other.

WHY IT'S SO TOUGH TO BE A GIRL
Nancy J. Perry

If girls are tougher and more resilient than boys, as many developmental experts insist, why do they so often seem to plunge deeper into unhappiness when they hit their teens? Adolescence--no picnic for anyone--is superficially harder on boys. Young women get raped; young men get killed. Girls attempt suicide more often than boys; boys more often succeed. Says Joy Dryfoos, author of *Adolescents at Risk*: "I think we've equalized the misery of growing up." But when things go wrong these days, the consequences for girls are often disastrous compared with earlier times, as reflected in rising sexual abuse and widespread teenage pregnancies, alcohol problems, and depression.

To some feminists, the answer is easy; when they hit their teens, girls begin to realize that women are not valued in society and grow quietly depressed at the thought of their futures. Maybe, but on the other hand, women have never had more opportunities. Many of the girls *Fortune* talked to for this story had *higher* aspirations and expectations than boys did. It wasn't the future that was making these girls miserable. It was the present.

At the root of much of the pain is lack of parental involvement. In a discussion with four boys and four girls at the Phoenix House drug rehabilitation center in Orange County, California, a reporter asked what one thing they would change about their lives. The boys gave four different replies, but the girls' answers were nearly identical. All yearned for better relationships with their families.

Even in the closest of families, being a teenage girl is scary. As most of them--and the experts as well--see it, the clear and present danger is boys. Says Dr. James Garbarino, president of the Erikson Institute for Advanced Study in Child Development in Chicago: "Sexist attitudes remain a major risk factor for girls. Date rape numbers testify to a climate of coercion." Many boys, he adds, feel that if a girl is just seductively dressed, she has lost the right to say no.

Don't believe it? Listen to what these 14 and 15-year-old girls, mostly white and lower middle class, had to say about their male peers during a weekly discussion session at the Newport Mesa, California, affiliate of Girls Incorporated--formerly Girls Clubs of America. "They pressure you. They get you drunk." "You have to be perfect for them." "They can change you. They get you into drugs." "They keep pushing and pushing. And if you care about them, you'll do anything for them. You want to believe it: someone loves me."

The fragile pubescent female psyche takes a further battering from the media. Sex spices everything from rock videos and talk shows to PG-13 movies and fast-food commercials. Veronica C. Garcia, principal of the New Futures School for pregnant and parenting teens in Albuquerque, New Mexico, fumed recently about a Taco Bell commercial that used women in scanty dresses to sell a fajita. Says Garcia: "We sell kids sex, but then we don't really want to talk to them about it."

Having been told repeatedly that they're sex objects, girls become even more subject to the usual teen anxieties about appearance. Today's specifications call for blonde and thin--no easy task, since most girls get bigger during adolescence. Many become anorexics or bulimics; a few rich ones get liposuction. Says Kristen Golden of the Ms. Foundation for Women: "Suddenly they need diets, even surgery. It's incredible. It's not, 'If you study, you can do this.' It's 'If you mutilate yourself, you can look like this.' We make their focus pleasing other people and physical beauty."

Pleasing others often translates into having sex; young teenage girls talk about the subject today with a candor that is mind-boggling even to thirtysomethings. By age 20, according to surveys by the Alan Guttmacher Institute, a nonprofit reproductive health research organization, some 44% of all girls in the U.S. and 63% of black girls, will become pregnant at least once. The institute does not track teen pregnancy rates by income level, but anecdotal evidence indicates that a fair number of white, middle-class, suburban kids are getting pregnant.

While the pregnancy rate among sexually active teens is dropping as more use contraceptives, the overall rate has remained constant for the past decade because teens are becoming sexually active at a younger age. Drawing on regular surveys, the Guttmacher Institute reports that in 1982, 19% of unmarried women age 15 had had intercourse; in 1988, the most recent year studied, 27% had. Result: The U.S. has one of the highest birthrates for 15- to 19-year olds among Western industrialized nations. Other surveys suggest that the rate of HIV-positive infection is growing rapidly among adolescent girls.

What can be done? Providing teenage girls and boys with greater information about--and access to-- birth control would doubtless help; roughly 80% of all teen pregnancies are unintended, according to experts. Better still to give younger girls the support they need to delay their first sexual experience. In the Will Power/Won't Power component of the Girls Incorporated Preventing Adolescent Pregnancy program, counselors help girls age 12 to 14 who come mainly from low-income families build assertiveness skills so they are able to say no because they don't feel emotionally ready for sex. In role-playing exercises, the girls act out ways of dealing with boys' advances; they also weigh alternatives--facing, for example, the likelihood that getting pregnant may force them to give up a shot at college.

Girls could also benefit from a wider variety of challenges than just the sexual. Says Martha Barcia, who is working with the Ms. Foundation to identify developmental programs available to girls throughout the U.S.: "The programs that girls like best are those that point to their strengths. It's better to say to a girl, 'You have an incredible talent in art, and we should encourage that,' than to say, 'It's a sin to have sex and that's it."

Are all-girl schools the answer? The verdict is unclear at best. Graduates of women's colleges make up a disproportionate number of the women in Congress and on Fortune 500 industrial and service company boards. Critics counter that most girls who attend single-sex schools are just putting off the day they will have to compete with boys in the real world.

One fact nobody disputes: many of the challenges girls face, from peer pressure and twisted cultural messages to wrongheaded classroom training--can be mitigated by the presence of caring, trusted adults who believe in them. For many--especially those without families or with families who don't know how to care--mentors can help. In Los Angeles a program called MOSTE (Motivating Our Students Through Experience) pairs up eighth- and ninth-grade girls, mostly from poor and minority households, with successful local businesswomen. These women work on building the girls' self-esteem, exposing them to a world they otherwise couldn't know. MOSTE also sponsors monthly programs in the schools on topics ranging from career strategy to etiquette.

Olga Romero, a 15-year-old Hispanic living in South Central Los Angeles, says her mentor, Marilyn Boyko, has made a big difference in her life. Boyko, a gregarious woman who runs her own special-events business, takes Olga to museums, movies, and fancy restaurants. Says Olga: "That's nice, since I'm used to Jack-in-the-Box and McDonald's. They brought me all these forks and spoons, and I didn't know how to eat. So I said, 'How do you eat this?' Marilyn taught me how to dress for the occasion, to put the napkin on my lap. I didn't know that. I've never done that before."

Better yet, Olga, whose grade point average rose from 1.2 to 3.5 during the past year, now plans to go to college and pursue a career. That's a change. Says she: "I wanted to get married at 16. Now I don't. I see all these ladies in MOSTE who can do anything they want because they aren't married and they have careers. I said, 'I want to be like them. I want to have a career, and then I can get married and have kids.'" The only drawback to the program, Olga says, is that there isn't one for boys.∎

NOTES

ACKNOWLEDGMENTS

pp. 11-13   From "An Invitation to Sociology" by Peter L. Berger. Copyright © 1963 by Peter L. Berger. Used by permission of Doubleday, a division of Bantam Doubleday Dell Publishing Group, Inc.

pp. 23-27   From *The Sociological Imagination* by C. Wright Mills. Copyright © 1959 by Oxford University Press, Inc.; renewed by Yaraslava Mills. Reprinted by permission of the publisher.

pp. 39-40   Excerpted from Thomas Sowell, *A World View of Cultural Diversity*. Published by permission of Transaction Publishers, from *Society*, Vol. 28, No. 4, pp. 37-43. Copyright © 1991 by Transaction Publishers.

pp. 63-64   "My Daughter Smokes" from *Living By the Word: Selected Writings 1973-1978*, Copyright © 1987 by Alice Walker, reprinted by permission of Harcourt Brace Jovanovich, Inc.

pp. 77-78   Excerpt from *Slim's Table* by Mitchell Duneier. Copyright © 1992. Reprinted by permission of the University of Chicago Press.

pp. 89-91   "Differential Association," by Donald R. Cressey from *Principles of Criminology* by Edwin H. Sutherland. Reprinted by permission of The Estate of Donald R. Cressey.

pp. 101-103   "Some Principles of Stratification," by Kingsley Davis and Wilbert E. Moore from *The American Sociological Review*, April 1945, Vol. 10, No. 2. Reprinted by permission of Kingsley Davis.

pp. 123-128   From *Unreliable Sources: A Guide to Dectecting Bias in News Media* by Martin A. Lee and Norman Solomon. Copyright © 1990 by Martin A. Lee and Norman Solomon. Published by arrangement with Carol Publishing Group. A Lyle Stuart Book.

pp. 139-140   Nancy J. Perry, "Why It's So Tough To Be A Girl," *Fortune*, August 10, 1992, pp. 82-84. Copyright © 1992 *Time Inc*. All rights reserved.